THIS BOOK BELONGS TO

....

BRAZIL

WRITTEN BY ANDREA GAYLE PEREIRA

ILLUSTRATED BY SASINI LIYANA GUNAWARDHANA

Ola, I'm Maria! I would love for you to join me on an exciting journey around my country, Brazil!

Salvador, Bahia

Together, let's discover some interesting facts on what makes my country and people so special and unique.

Atlantic Ocean

Brazil is located in South America and it is the largest country on the continent. Its various landscapes and tropical climate allow for different activities to take place all year round.

There are over 200 million people who live here and our national language is Portuguese.

Our capital city is Brasilia. However, the bustling and stunning, Rio De Janeiro is the most popular city in the country.

Its beautiful natural wonders, tourist attractions and entertainment offer a bounty of experiences for all its visitors.

Our biggest and most awaited festival of the year is called Carnival. Thousands of people from all over the world gather to celebrate this big fun-filled parade of colourful costumes, dancing, samba music and yummy food.

It has been dubbed "the greatest show on earth".

Christ the Redeemer is Brazil's prized landmark.
It is a religious symbol that represents the Christian
faith of our people.

It took nine years to build and stands 98 feet tall on
Mount Corcovado in Rio.

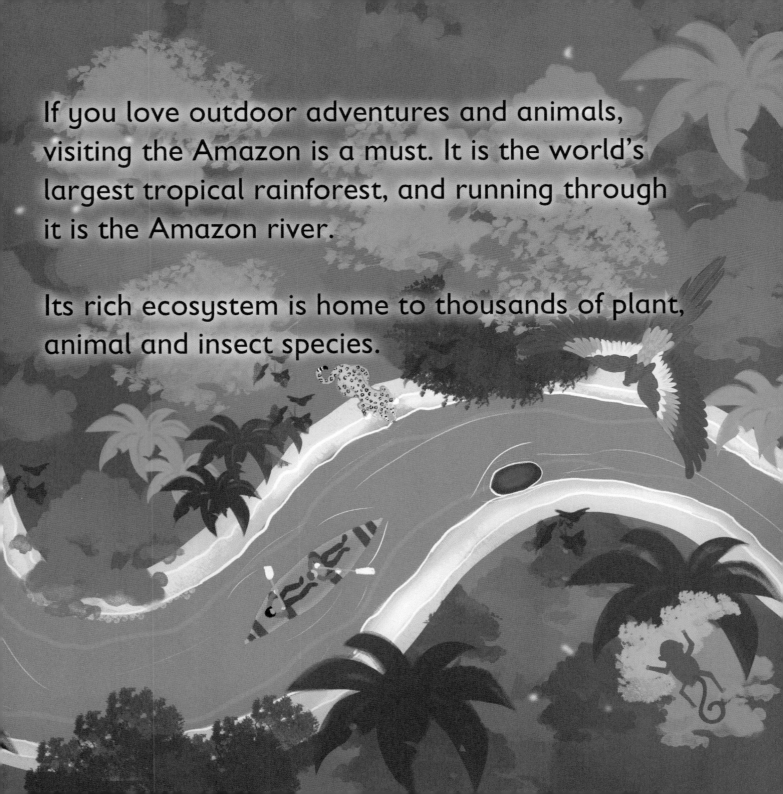

If you love outdoor adventures and animals, visiting the Amazon is a must. It is the world's largest tropical rainforest, and running through it is the Amazon river.

Its rich ecosystem is home to thousands of plant, animal and insect species.

Anaconda

Capybara

Giant River Otter

Black Caiman

Piranha

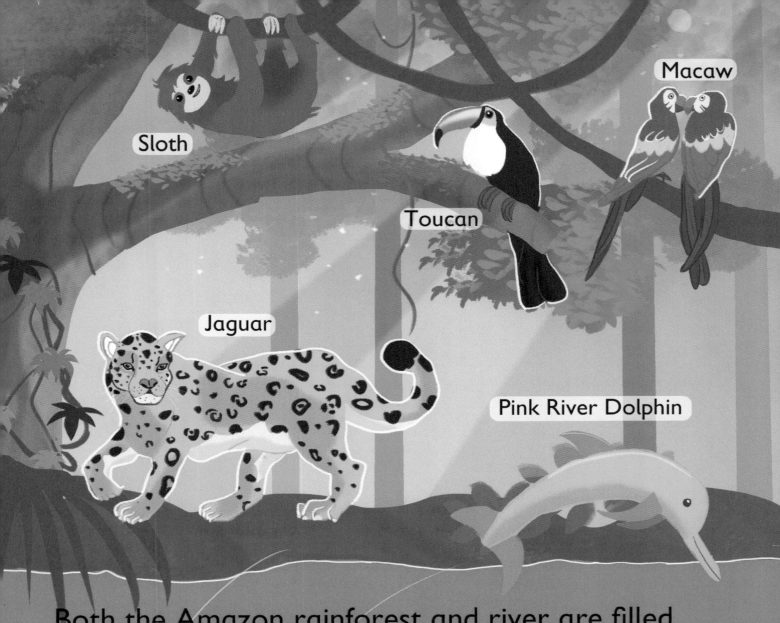

Both the Amazon rainforest and river are filled with all sorts of fascinating creatures, from the most beautiful birds to the most ferocious fish in the world.

We Brazilians love the sun, sea and sand.
Our beautiful golden sand beaches are among
the most beautiful in the world.

Ipanema Beach, Rio De Janeiro

Sitting on the Atlantic ocean with super long coastlines, there are over 2000 beaches to choose from!

Capoeira is Brazil's own form of martial arts. It was developed hundreds of years ago by slaves who wanted to disguise practising their fight moves.

What makes it unique is its combination of music, dance, self-defence and acrobatics. Today, it is a national pride and is taught all over the world.

When it comes to football, we eat, sleep and breathe the sport.

You see people with footballs everywhere you go and it is all we ever talk about. To us, it is more than just a game. It is part of our culture and way of life.

Iguazu Falls are on many people's lists of places to see. The waterfalls are one of the largest and most beautiful in the world. Located on the border between Brazil and Argentina, the exquisite waterfalls divide into 275 separate falls.

The word *Iguazu* means 'great water' in the local language.

Now that you have learnt about Brazil, I do hope you would come someday for a visit and experience the wonders of this place for yourself.

There are so many things to see and do, I guarantee you will have an experience of a lifetime!
Till next time, tchau!

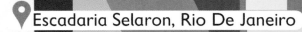
Escadaria Selaron, Rio De Janeiro

Printed in Great Britain
by Amazon

40561178R00016

The Queen's Horse

Gift Of The Mounties

Nora Hickson Kelly

For Tamara,
with best wishes.
Nora Hickson Kelly

Golden Dog Press

Ottawa – Canada

1996

Canadian Cataloguing in Publication Data

Kelly, Nora (Nora Hickson)
    The Queen's Horse – Gift Of The Mounties

ISBN 0-919614-69-8

1. Burmese (Horse)–Fiction.
2. Royal Canadian Mounted Police–Fiction.
3. Elizabeth II, Queen of Great Britain, 1926–Fiction.
I. Title.

PS8521.E536B87 1996   C813'.54   C96-900731-0
PR9199.3.K44B87 1996

Design by The Gordon Creative Group, Ottawa, Canada.

Printed in Canada.

Distributed by:
    Oxford University Press Canada
    70 Wynford Drive
    Don Mills, ON, Canada, M3C 1J9
    Phone: 416-441-2941, Fax: 416-444-0427

The Golden Dog Press wishes to express its appreciation to The Canada Council and the Ontario Arts Council for current and past support of its publishing programme.

To my husband with gratitude
for his valuable help.

Part One
Tammy's Blackie

Chapter 1

A Foal Is Born

Tammy leaned forward in the saddle and patted her pony's neck.

"You've given me a good ride, Jenny," she said. "Now it's time to go home." She pressed her heels against the pony's sides.

Jenny set out at a gallop over the high flatland that overlooked the Cypress Hills and the many valleys below. Tammy's open windbreaker flapped like yellow wings in the spring breeze. Her long brown hair blew straight out behind her.

Jenny slowed to a trot as Tammy guided her downhill. When they came to a gate of the side-hill pasture, the pony stopped. Tammy leaned over and lifted a big wire ring that fastened the gate to a strong fence post. Still without getting off her pony, she opened the gate, rode through, closed the gate, and slipped the wire ring back in place. The girl and the pony moved on, again at a slow pace downhill.

Suddenly Tammy saw a big dark form on the ground near a stand of pine trees. She knew it must be one of the ranch mares. She also knew that this was the time of year when the foals were born. Perhaps the mare was about to give birth.

Guiding Jenny closer, Tammy saw that she was right. A black mare with bulging sides lay stretched out on a patch of dried grass. The grass was flattened by her struggles.

The girl knew that when a mare was due to foal, her father and Scottie aimed to put her in the big box stall in the stable. That way, if the mare had problems, the men would be there to help. Tammy thought fast. Should she gallop home to tell the men? Or was it too late?

Then the mare gave a great heave, as if trying to expel the foal. It was too late to go home! So what should she do?

"Tammy Brown!" she seemed to hear her mother saying. "You're not able to help the mare. Come home at once!"

Then it was her father's voice she seemed to hear. "Tammy," it said, "remember you are the wrangler's daughter. Stay with the mare!"

Quickly Tammy slid from the saddle, dropping the reins over Jenny's head so she wouldn't wander away. Then she hurried to the mare.

The big black animal gave another heave. Then she relaxed her muscles. She lifted her head and looked back over her shoulder as if she expected to see something. But she didn't see what she seemed to expect. Head down again. Another heave. Relax. Head up and look back again.

At the next heave, Tammy saw two small yellowish hooves come out from the mare's body. Next came a small nose.

"Good girl," Tammy said, just as she had heard her father say. "You're doing fine."

Then the mare gave another heave, and Tammy saw the foal's head appear.

"One more push," she said. "Good girl!"

The mare no longer lifted her head and looked back. She lay flat and gave the biggest heave of all.

sacks he had thrown in before leaving the ranch. Minx put her head close to the foal, and snuffled as if she wanted it to know she would stay with it.

"You sit here and keep the wee creature from moving," Scottie said to Tammy. "I'll drive slowly, so Minx can follow us."

Tammy climbed into the truck. Settling herself on the floor, she cradled the foal's head in her lap. Carefully she pulled one of the sacks from under the foal, and tucked it around the still-damp body.

"There, there," she murmured, as if it were a baby. "Soon you'll be safe and warm at home."

Scottie started the truck and looked back to make sure everything was in order. Then, very slowly, he drove back down to the ranch, sometimes stopping to give Minx a rest.

The truck pulled up to the big stable, built of logs, painted white, and topped with a red roof. It looked much like all the other buildings at the ranch. Dave Brown came out to meet them just as Scottie was carrying the foal into the stable. The wrangler chuckled to see Tammy and Minx following close behind, side by side. The girl and the mare looked as if neither would let the other go first.

Chapter 2
A Pure Black Foal

Scottie carried the foal to a big box stall that had walls of wide boards. The stall had a door made in two parts. The bottom half could be closed while the top was left open. He placed the foal on a heap of straw that Dave had put there.

The foal immediately struggled to its feet. It wobbled as before, and its ears still drooped. Minx walked up to it, and licked it so hard that it lost its balance and flopped down again.

As it struggled to its feet once more, Tammy knelt beside it. She leaned close so that if it fell again, her body would break its fall. But the foal kept its wobbly legs wide apart, and was able to stay up.

A few moments later it began pushing its tiny head against Tammy's side.

"See, it's stronger already!" the girl exclaimed to the men. She got to her feet and stepped back to have a better look. The foal staggered after her and kept nudging her. "And it knows me!" Tammy exclaimed with pleasure. "It's smart! Small but smart, Scottie!"

"Small, right enough! No much bigger than a jack rabbit." Scottie chuckled. "But she's not very smart! She's looking for her first meal, and the poor wee filly foal thinks you're her mother."

Tammy turned the foal around and guided her to the mare's udder. "This is your mother," she said. "Minx, not me."

She held the foal's head in place. But even after several tries it failed to get hold of a teat. Once or twice it got hold of one of Tammy's fingers, and sucked strongly until the girl took her finger away.

"This little filly foal is smart enough to know what to do," she said, frowning at Scottie. "The trouble is, she's getting the wrong thing in her mouth. "

At last the foal got hold of the right thing, and suckled contentedly. Tammy backed away slowly, ready to help again if she was needed. But the foal stayed up on its wobbly legs and kept on suckling.

Dave Brown had been silent, pleased that his daughter was taking such an interest in the new foal. Now he spoke.

"We'd better go in for supper now," he said.

Tammy followed the men, but only after giving Minx and her foal a few gentle goodbye pats.

A few minutes later they all sat at the big table in the ranch kitchen enjoying Susan Brown's meat loaf and mashed potatoes. Tammy couldn't stop talking about the new foal.

"You've seen dozens of new foals, " her mother said. "Last year you even saw one being born. But I've never heard you talk about any of them like this."

"This one's different," Tammy said.

"Different is right," Scottie teased. "She's no much bigger than yon cat." He nodded toward the big tabby sitting near the stove. "I doubt she'll grow big enough to pass the inspection committee when she's six months old."

Tammy felt a lump in her throat. "What will happen to her if she's too small, daddy?"

"The Mounted Police will sell her," Dave Brown answered. "But don't worry! In all the years we've had the ranch, only two foals have been too small. This one might grow up to be a fine mare. "

"If she doesn't," Tammy asked, "could we buy her? In a few years Jennie will be too old for me to ride, and by then this filly will be just the right age for me to ride."

Her father's usual good humour seemed to be wearing thin. "For heaven's sake, Tammy, forget the foal and get on with your supper!" he said.

"Please do!" Susan Brown smiled as she brought on her daughter's favorite apple crunch desert. "After supper you can show me the foal that's different from all the others."

When the men went out to the stable to see how Minx and her foal were getting on, Tammy and her mother went, too.

Tammy was glad to see that the little creature was steadier on her feet, although her ears were still droopy. It was easy to see that she had drunk a lot of her mother's milk: her little round belly looked as tight as a drum. Minx had licked her dry, and her coat was all fuzzy. It didn't seem quite as dark, though, as when it was wet and shiny.

The little foal walked toward the visitors, still wobbling a bit. When she came to Tammy she stopped and nuzzled her. Tammy hugged her around the neck.

"I see what you mean," Susan Brown said. "By the way, Dave, is it too soon for you to know what colour she'll be when she's bigger?"

Tammy watched her father carefully examine the foal. She knew how important colour was. The mounties needed black horses for their Musical Ride, so everyone hoped that each new foal would be black. Most of the Ride horses had some white on their faces or legs, so a pure black was special.

As Dave finished looking over the dark little body, he was smiling.

"We're in luck!" he said. "She's all black! She hasn't any white hairs, and there's no hint of brown anywhere. Even the ring around her muzzle is as dark as can be. She'll probably grow up to be as black as coal."

"We surely are in luck!" Susan Brown smiled at her husband. A few moments later she went back to the house.

Tammy stayed with the men. While they put hay in the manger and heaped more straw under and around the mare, Tammy fed her a pail of warm bran mash. Then she gave the foal another gentle rub-down, this time with a soft cloth.

When the men had finished their chores, Tammy followed them to the door of the stall. The foal followed her as if it expected to go where she went.

"You can't come with me," Tammy said, turning the foal around. "There's your mother, and this big box stall is your home for now."

She slipped through the partly closed bottom half of the door. She waited to see the foal go back to Minx and begin to suckle. "Goodnight, Blackie," she whispered. Then she hurried out to catch up with the men.

"Blackie is having a bedtime snack," she told them.

"Blackie, is it?" her father said. "Well, I guess that name is as good as any, at least till the mounties give her an official name this fall."

Scottie shook his head. "I doubt if the inspection committee will recommend that we keep her," he said. "She'll never grow big enough."

Later that evening, Tammy sat in the kitchen with her parents. They were all reading, but Tammy couldn't keep her mind on her library book. She was glad that Scottie had gone to his room, so he wasn't there to tease her. She began to pester her father about buying Blackie if she didn't grow big enough for the mounties."

"For goodness sake, Tamara, give your father a rest!" Susan Brown said sharply. "Just be glad you can have Blackie as long as she's here on the ranch!"

Tammy knew that her mother used her full name, Tamara, only when she was cross or worried. She was sorry she had upset her.

"I am glad," she said. "And I'm glad she's going to be pure black. That way, if she does grow big enough for the mounties, she's sure to get into the Musical Ride. She's too smart to be an ordinary police horse."

Tammy took up her book again, but her mind was in the foaling stall with Blackie. She put the book down, and went to her room to get the diary she had used since her eleventh birthday two months ago.

Seating herself at the big kitchen table, she wrote in it.

"Saturday, May 19, 1962. Today I saw Blackie being born. She is the most beautiful and the smartest foal ever born here on the RCMP ranch at Fort Walsh in southern Saskatchewan. Her mother is Minx." She paused.

"Which stallion is Blackie's father, daddy?" she asked.

Dave looked up from his newspaper. "Faux Pas," he answered. "He's the one I showed you in the corral a while back. He used to be a famous

English race horse. Before the Mounted Police bought him, he won the Ascot Gold Vase. In 1951, I think it was."

"Ascot!" Tammy's mother looked up from her book. "That's where the queen goes every year to watch the races!"

Tammy's eyes popped wide open. "So I suppose the queen was there watching when Blackie's father won the Gold Vase!" she exclaimed.

"The present queen didn't get to be queen till 1952," her father said. "But she always loved horses, so probably she was there in 1951 with her parents, King George VI and Queen Elizabeth."

"I told you Blackie is special!" Tammy almost shouted.

After asking her father how to spell "Faux Pas", she turned back to her diary. But even after she had finished writing in it, she could only think of Blackie and her famous father. Now she was even more sure that Blackie could do well in the Musical Ride.

That night Tammy dreamed about a tiny black filly foal with a fuzzy coat and floppy ears. She pranced ahead of a lot of beautiful black horses while they performed the Musical Ride. Somewhere to one side, the queen sat on her throne, smiling and clapping.

Chapter 3
Tammy's Blackie

About six o'clock the next morning, Tammy awoke to hear her father and Scottie talking in the kitchen. Quickly she dressed in her week-end brown slacks and green sweater, and hurried to join them. She knew that as soon as they had finished their coffee they would go out to feed the horses. It was too early in the year for the horses to find enough good grass in the pasture. So every morning and evening the men gave them hay and oats in the feeding corral, where they stayed every night.

She knew, too, that they would go first to see Minx and her foal. She put on her yellow windbreaker, ready to go with them.

"May I give Blackie a little sugar?" she asked her father.

He nodded. "But only a little loose sugar. No lumps. They could choke her."

Tammy spooned a little sugar from the sugar bowl into waxed paper. She put it in the pocket of her windbreaker, and went out with the men.

They found Minx and Blackie standing in a corner of the box stall. Minx was licking the foal so hard that her tongue made a scraping sound. Blackie had to brace herself to keep on her feet, but she didn't seem to mind.

Minx gave a soft whinney and walked toward the visitors. Dave patted her neck.

"You've given us a lovely black filly," he said.

"Too bad she's too small," Scottie said.

"Anyway," Tammy said, "she's beautiful." She stroked the foal's fuzzy neck. "She's smart, too. Today she's standing up without wobbling. She's holding her ears up, too. And if she doesn't grow big enough for the mounties, we'll keep her.

"We'll see about that later," Dave answered. "Right now Scottie and I have to feed about ninety horses. Scottie, you get the hay for Minx. Then come and help me."

As soon as the men had left, Tammy emptied the sugar into her hand and held it to Blackie's nose. The foal licked it, then went back to Minx and began to suckle.

Tammy could see that Blackie was interested only in suckling. She leaned over and gave the foal a hug.

"We're lucky it's Sunday," she said. "I'll see you after breakfast."

When Tammy came back, she found Minx and her foal out in the foaling corral. She climbed to the top rail of the pole fence and watched them.

Minx paced back and forth as if she wanted to get back to the freedom of the pasture. Blackie soon grew tired of following her. She pricked up her ears at everything she heard or saw – a dog barking, Scottie driving the tractor, sparrows flying past.

When Scottie brought a pail of bran mash and held it for Minx, Blackie put her head in the pail, too. Then she ran about, trying to shake the wet mash from her face. Tammy jumped down and wiped her clean with a tissue from her pocket.

"You'll spoil that foal," Scottie said sharply.

Tammy pretended not to hear. As he left, she made a face behind his back.

After lunch Tammy went out again. She beamed with pride as the day-old foal ran round and round. She laughed as Blackie tried to jump over her own shadow. But the girl held her breath when the foal ran after a sparrow and almost scraped her soft little nose on the rough fence rails.

At last Blackie grew tired and lay down at her mother's feet to rest in the warm spring sunshine. Tammy knew she might as well leave then. But before she went, she waved away the flies that settled on the foal and made her twitch.

"Never mind, Blackie," Tammy said before leaving the corral. "When your tail grows longer, you'll be able to switch away the flies like your mother does."

In the evening Tammy went out again. Now Blackie and Minx were back in the box stall.

"Goodnight, Blackie," Tammy said as she put her arms around the foal's neck once more.

The next day, Monday, Tammy got up very early. She wanted to visit Blackie before the car pool lady came to drive her to the little school at Meadowlands about eight kilometres to the south.

This time while the foal licked up the sugar from Tammy's hand, she looked up at the girl from time to time. Tammy felt sure that the foal was beaming out her loving thanks. When the sugar was all gone, the foal snuffled at the girl's sugar pocket. When Tammy moved away, Blackie followed her to the door of the box stall. She still nuzzled the pocket and nudged the girl with her nose.

After school Tammy took out more sugar to Blackie. This time when the foal had licked the last bit of sugar, she nipped Tammy's hand.

"Teeth!" the girl exclaimed. She parted the foal's lips. "Two at the top, and two at the bottom! And you're only two days old!"

As Dave Brown explained at supper time, it was not strange for a foal to have a few teeth even when it was born. Most foals had four teeth by the time they were ten days old. Still, he admitted when Tammy pressed him, Blackie was well ahead for her age.

"Small but smart! That's what she is," Tammy said. "And I'm glad she's small. This way she might be mine someday."

It seemed to the Browns and Scottie that Tammy already owned Blackie.

The next morning the girl got up very early again. She knew Scottie was going to turn Minx and her foal loose so they could go to the pasture with the other horses.

While Dave and Scottie fed the horses in the feeding corral, Tammy went to the stable.

"Here, Minx," she said, holding out an apple. "It's to thank you for having Blackie." Minx ate it in two bites.

By this time the foal was nuzzling Tammy's sugar pocket. As before, when she had eaten the sugar, she nudged Tammy for more, and followed her to the door of the stall.

'I hope you won't forget me when you get out with the other horses," Tammy said as she went out.

Scottie had already saddled Jenny. When he rode up to let out the mare and the foal, he brought the pony so that Tammy could ride with him.

The main herd of the ninety-odd horses had already started moving away from the complex of corrals. Soon they were climbing the hill to the side-hill pasture. In the lead trotted the few three-year-olds that had not yet been taken to the Mounted Police stables at Regina. About fifty two-year-olds and yearlings followed them closely. Trailing the others were a lot of mares and foals, and about a dozen mares without foals. Most of the horses were black with bits of white here and there, but some were brown.

Blackie followed her black mother, but her little legs slowed her down as she climbed the hill. She and Minx were last in line.

"She's not quite three days old," Tammy said to Scottie as they rode not far behind. "She's too small to climb hills."

"She's too small, period," Scottie said as Blackie trudged after Minx through the gate.

He closed the gate and fastened it by slipping the wire ring over the fence post, all without getting off his horse. Then he and Tammy rode back to the ranch for breakfast.

By the time Tammy got home from school, Scottie had gone to bring the horses back to the feeding corral. She dashed into the house, calling, "Hi, mom!" as she ran past. Quickly she changed her clothes, drank the milk her mother had set out, and spooned a bit of sugar into waxed paper.

She knew that Minx and Blackie would go to the feeding corral with the others. She hurried there and saw the first horses arriving.

Blackie must have been very tired. She was last again. As soon as Minx stood still to eat some hay, the foal began to suckle. Neither of them paid any attention to the girl who had so eagerly run out to meet them.

"Let them eat first." Scottie's voice was soothing, as if he knew how Tammy felt. "You can help me with the oats.."

She went with him to the oat shed and held open the sacks while he filled them with his big scoop. By the time he had carried them to the corral and emptied them into the wooden feeding boxes, Blackie had had enough milk.

Tammy called her. The foal went over and nuzzled her sugar pocket.

"Look!" Tammy shouted. "She remembers me!"

"Aye, she does that," Scottie laughed. "She still thinks you're her other mother."

"That's okay with me!" Tammy smiled as she took out the packet of sugar.

CHAPTER 4
Thunder Storm

By the end of June, the horses had been moved to the summer pasture, which now had plenty of good grass. By then, too, Tammy's summer holidays had begun. Every afternoon she went to the pasture to see her pet.

Susan Brown was happy that Tammy was so interested in Blackie. But one very hot day she wished that her daughter had not been so fond of the foal.

After lunch Tammy was in the kitchen, making up a packet of sugar.

"You shouldn't go to the summer pasture today," Susan said as she hurried into the kitchen. "The radio just warned everyone about a severe thunder storm heading this way."

Tammy looked out of the big window above the sink. Dark clouds had formed in the northern sky, and were giving way to darker ones. Even as she watched, the clouds darkened and grew, grew and darkened.

"I have to go, mom," she said. "I don't want Blackie to be alone in her first thunder storm."

"Tamara!" her mother said sharply. "Minx will be with her!"

"Sorry, mom, but I have to go," Tammy said. She left the sugar on the table and dashed out.

"I wish your father was here to stop you!" Susan called after her. But Dave and Scottie were out mending fences.

Tammy ran toward the stable. She looked up and saw dark clouds lying low in the northern sky. The sun was still pouring its searing heat from the clear part of the great sky dome. Maybe she could reach Blackie before the storm broke!

Dashing into Jenny's corral, she snatched the pony's bridle from its nail on a nearby post, and slid it over Jenny's head. No time for a saddle! She got a toe-hold on the fence and scrambled up on Jenny's bare back. Kicking the pony with her heels, she guided her out of the corral, across the valley floor, and up to the summer pasture.

When she reached the gate she was afraid to get off Jenny in case she couldn't get back on. Grabbing Jenny's mane, she leaned sideways as far as she dared. Then she carefully lifted the ring from its fence post. She had never opened a gate while riding bareback, but she was able to stay on as she pushed it open. After getting safely through, she kept a firm grip on Jenny's mane as she leaned sideways again while she pushed the gate closed and dropped the ring over the post.

Madly she galloped to the place where the horses often went on the hottest days. She found the mares there, in the shade of a stand of poplars. They were near Battle Creek, the swift-flowing stream that ran through several of the pastures and the feeding corral. The horses stood in pairs, heads to tails, flicking away the flies with their tails. The foals were not with them!

Tammy galloped on to the buffalo stones, but the foals weren't there, either. As she hurried deeper into the pasture, the sun went out of sight, and the sky grew almost black. She heard faint rumbles of thunder, then louder rumbles. Suddenly, sharp flashes of lightning zig-zagged down to earth. A great clap of thunder followed. Then came the rain. It soaked Tammy and Jenny in a few moments, and bounced up from the earth like hail.

Tammy was used to thunder storms. Although she didn't like to get soaking wet, she wasn't afraid. The trouble was, she could imagine how frightened Blackie must be. Then she saw her, huddled with the other foals under one of the biggest trees in the pasture.

The girl knew that sheltering under a big tree during a thunder storm was the worst thing to do. She knew that lightning always strikes the highest thing in its path. She galloped up to the foals, shouting and trying to chase them out. They were already dripping wet, as if they had been caught in the heavy rain before they ran for cover. They refused to leave the tree.

Tammy slid down from Jenny, letting the reins hang down so the pony would stay. She got behind the foal and tried to push her out into the open. Blackie braced her legs and would not move.

"You stupid, stubborn foal!" Tammy shouted. "You could be struck by lightning if you stay here! And if I stay, I could be struck, too!"

She stayed anyway. The dripping wet girl hugged and stroked the dripping, shivering foal. The other foals came close. As the rain, the lightning and the thunder continued, Tammy kept whispering to Blackie that she had nothing to fear. After a while, she herself began to believe it.

Suddenly a zig-zag of white flame shot down to earth. It hit a big tree only a few yards away. Almost at the same time a deafening clap of thunder rent the air. The tree split in two and fell with a crash. Jenny galloped away.

For a moment the rain eased up and everything was quiet. Then it poured down again, pounding the earth harder than ever. As the frightened foals milled about, Tammy got behind Blackie and tried to push her out from under the big tree.

"Our tree could be next!" the girl shouted. "Go on, Blackie! Please!"

The foal still refused to move.

By now the rain was falling in torrents, even through the leafy branches overhead. It seemed as if a great dam in the sky had overflowed. Tammy knew she could never get Blackie to go out in that downpour. She stopped trying, and began to tremble with fear.

"Oh, Blackie," she moaned, throwing her wet arms around the foal's wet neck. She pressed her face into the soggy black hair. "We might get killed here! But I can't go and leave you."

Blackie made soft little noises and nuzzled the girl. The other foals pressed in closer as if they, too, felt her distress. They all huddled together and waited. Lightning flashed and thunder cracked. Rain beat through the branches and all around them.

At last the storm ended as suddenly as it had begun. The rain stopped falling. The clouds parted and the sun broke through. Wet leaves and grass sparkled in the sunshine.

Tammy gave Blackie a few gentle pats as she stared out at the changed scene. She could hardly believe they were safe. She moved through the foals and out from under the tree, glad to feel the warmth of the sun on her soaking wet hair and clothes. The foals, too, left the tree, and tried to shake themselves dry.

Luckily, Jenny had not galloped far, perhaps because she was afraid of tripping over the dangling reins. Tammy led her to the fallen tree, and used it as a mounting block to help her scramble to the pony's wet, slippery back.

As they set out for home, Blackie and the other foals followed. When they reached the mares, Tammy waited to see Blackie run to Minx and begin to suckle. Then she hurried home to let her own mother know that she, too, was safe.

Chapter 5
Blackie's Early Training

A few days after the storm, Blackie was six weeks old. Tammy wanted to begin her training.

"She's much too young," Dave said. But he let Tammy choose one of the white cotton training halters he put on foals when they were old enough.

Tammy chose the cleanest one. She took it, with several packets of sugar, to the summer pasture.

"Come, Blackie," she called, and the foal went to meet her.

Tammy thought that if she held the sugar in her left hand, she could use her right hand to slip the halter over the foal's head.

It didn't work out that way. Blackie was so frightened that she ran away and wouldn't come back. Tammy tried again the next day. And the next. And the next. At last she was able to slip the halter over the pretty black head. The foal kicked up her heels and dashed away, shaking her head and trying to get rid of the thing that felt so strange. After several days, though, she grew used to it, and went to meet Tammy as usual.

Next the girl snapped a halter rope to the strap under the foal's chin, and tried to lead her. But again Blackie grew very frightened, so Tammy let her loose.

Only after many tries and much petting, Blackie let herself be led with the halter rope. Tammy began by walking backward, and holding out sugar in her free hand. After the foal was used to being led that way, Tammy was able to lead her the usual way, with the foal walking behind her.

Within a few weeks, Blackie let Tammy tie her to a tree. She learned to stand still while the girl wiped her with a soft cloth and, later, with a soft brush. Still later, she let Tammy comb her sprouting mane and forelock.

"You're beautiful," Tammy said one day as she stood back and looked at her pet. When she turned around, she saw they had a visitor.

"You have a fine foal, Tammy," he said. "She's unusually small, but she is a beauty."

"Thank you, Commissioner Wood," Tammy smiled.

S.T. Wood, who used to be the mounties' commissioner, had known Tammy since she was a baby. The girl knew that even before he was commissioner, he thought the mounties should use black horses instead of brown ones. He wanted black because the mounties' scarlet tunics would show up better against black. When he became commissioner, he ordered the mounties to buy only black horses. When they couldn't get enough suitable blacks, he decided they should breed their own.

Soon the mounties set up the breeding ranch at Fort Walsh. They built it on the site of Old Fort Walsh, which the old time mounties had built in the early days. For the new fort they used pine logs from the nearby woods, just as the early mounties had used such logs for the old fort.

When Commissioner Wood retired, the RCMP made him a special constable, without pay. After that he watched over the breeding program, about which he cared so much.

Tammy had got to know Commissioner Wood because he and Mrs. Wood went to live at Fort Walsh every summer. They lived in a red-roofed log house painted white like all the other buildings there.

As Tammy's holiday weeks passed, Commissioner Wood often came to see how the foal was getting on. Her black coat now had a sheen very different from her baby fuzz. She was growing bigger, but was still much smaller than the other foals. By the end of July she had eight front teeth, so she could nibble pieces of apple, and even eat cubes of sugar.

Tammy used such tidbits to teach the foal a difficult trick. The foal had to let Tammy lift one of the front feet. She didn't know how to stand on only three legs, even though Tammy kept placing her back legs where they would keep her from wobbling. At last, though, after lots of stroking and hugging as well as tidbits, Blackie learned to lift her left front foot.

Proudly, Tammy showed her parents and Commissioner Wood what the foal could do. But she was even more eager to show Scottie. One afternoon she learned that he had to take a team and wagon to the summer pasture to set out salt blocks for the horses. She asked him to come and see Blackie lift her foot.

"She's too young to do tricks," Scottie said. But he went anyway.

No matter how many tidbits Tammy gave the foal, she wouldn't let Tammy lift her foot.

"I told you she's too young," Scottie laughed. He was still chuckling as he climbed into the wagon and drove away.

"You bad foal!" Tammy scolded. "You know you can do it."

Once more she took Blackie's left foot in her hand. "Lift!" she ordered. This time the foal let Tammy lift her foot.

"Scottie! Scottie!" Tammy shouted. But he was too far away to hear her.

A few days later, Blackie let Tammy lift each foot in turn in exchange for tidbits. At last she grew so used to it that sometimes she lifted her left front foot by herself, as if asking for a tidbit. Tammy always gave her one if she had any left. So that trick became a habit with the foal, still not three months old.

Early in August, RCMP Inspector Collins came from Regina to inspect the ranch. He, Commissioner Wood and Wrangler Dave went to the pasture to check the horses. Tammy and Blackie were just finishing their day's lessons.

The girl let the foal loose and walked over to the men. Blackie followed, and stood nuzzling Tammy's tidbit pocket. When she got nothing, she gave Tammy a nudge and lifted her left front foot. Tammy gave her the last bit of apple.

"What an unusual foal!" the inspector said.

"This is the one I've been telling you about, sir," Dave said. "She's very intelligent and good-natured. Better still, she's perfectly black, with perfect conformation."

"She's all that," Commissioner Wood agreed.

Tammy knew that perfect conformation was something special. It meant that everything about the foal's appearance matched with what horsemen thought was a perfect horse of her kind. The girl felt a thrill of pride that her father and Commissioner Wood agreed with what she had known from the beginning: Blackie was perfect!

"Unfortunately," Dave went on, "I'm afraid she's too small for the police."

"Maybe she'll grow big enough," the inspector said. "We don't often get a foal that's so nearly perfect."

"If she doesn't grow big enough for the mounties, inspector," Tammy said, "would you let my dad buy her?"

"I can't promise that," Inspector Collins answered. "The government has a rule that Mounted Police horses must be sold by auction. That way, everybody has a chance to buy them. And as this foal's father is the famous Faux Pas, there might be people willing to pay more than your father could afford."

Tammy looked at her father, but he didn't say anything.

"Anyway," the inspector went on, "we've got much bigger worries than what to do with this foal. After I leave, your father will tell you what I mean."

The news Dave Brown told his wife, Scottie and Tammy did indeed make Blackie seem less important. The mounties had heard that the government was going to order them to get rid of their horses to save money. If that happened, the mounties would have to give up the ranch. Then Dave Brown and Scottie would lose their jobs. Nobody could guess what would happen after that.

Tammy felt a big lump in her throat. What about Blackie? she thought. But she didn't ask it aloud. She didn't want to upset her parents any more than they were already upset.

That night she couldn't get to sleep. She began to cry, burying her face in the pillow so that her parents wouldn't hear her. But her mother heard her, just as she used to hear Tammy when she was a baby. Susan tiptoed into her daughter's room.

"Don't worry, dear," she said. She sat on the bed and leaned over to put her arms around the sobbing girl. "Whatever happens, your father and you and I will still have one another."

Tammy caught her breath. "I know, and I'm glad of it," she said. She sat up in bed and returned her mother's hug. "But I don't want to lose Blackie."

"There, there!" Her mother soothed her just as Tammy had soothed the new born foal in the back of the truck. "Things will work out."

Tammy couldn't imagine how, but at last she said goodnight and slid down into bed.

Susan tucked the covers around her as gently as Tammy had tucked the gunny sack around the still-damp little foal. Then she tiptoed out.

Chapter 6
The Musical Ride

"There's something we must remember," Dave said at lunch time the next day. "It's only a rumour that the mounties will have to give up their horses."

The other three nodded.

"Oh, yes!" Tammy smiled. She felt much better.

"Also," Susan said, "we must enjoy what we have now. Dave. you tell Tammy what we have planned."

The plan was wonderful. The Musical Ride was to perform at the Regina exhibition one weekend at the end of August. The Browns would drive the 430 kilometres to Regina and would spend that weekend with Tammy's Aunt Doris and Uncle Jim Hanson. They would all go to see the Ride.

"Wow!" Tammy exclaimed. "I've only seen bits on television. It will be great to see the whole show."

A few weeks later, the Browns drove into the Hansons' driveway. Soon Tammy had another pleasant surprise. Inspector Collins had given Uncle Jim three extra tickets for the Saturday afternoon show. The Browns could sit with the Hansons in the visitors' section of the grandstand. They would have a splendid view of everything.

Before the show started, Dave took Susan and Tammy to see the horses and riders. They were waiting in the shade behind the grandstand.

Tammy gasped as she saw the thirty-two big black horses standing in eight rows with four horses in each row. The horses' manes and forelocks had been clipped off. Their necks and heads looked as sleek and shiny as their bodies. Their white headbands made their lovely black heads look even blacker.

At each horse's head stood a mountie wearing a brilliant scarlet tunic, and holding his horse's bridle reins. The black of the horses made the scarlet tunics look more brilliant than it really was. Each mountie held a bamboo lance about two and a half metres long, topped with a small pointed red and white pennon.

Every piece of brown leather shone as if it had been polished for hours: saddles, bridles, the Mounties' high boots, the bands on their Stetson hats. Every piece of metal gleamed: spurs, tunic buttons, stirrups, even the smallest buckles on the saddles and bridles.

"It's all so splendid!" Tammy gasped. "And the horses are so big! My head isn't even as high as their shoulders!" Then she was silent. She was thinking of Blackie. Maybe Scottie was right when he said Blackie could never grow big enough for the mounties. If that was true, and if the mounties kept using horses so her father kept his job, and if he had enough money … oh, if only she could have Blackie for her very own, she'd be the happiest girl in the world!

The inspector in charge of the Ride took the three visitors up and down the rows of horses and mounties. He didn't forget his own horse, standing apart from the others. Then it was time for the Browns to leave.

They found their seats beside the Hansons in the centre section, a few rows from the front. On the field just below them they could see the RCMP band. The bandsmen, like the Ride mounties, wore scarlet tunics, and their brass instruments shone in the bright sunshine.

In the first and second rows of seats below the Browns and the Hansons, Tammy saw mounties in blue uniforms wearing peaked caps trimmed with gold braid. With them were women in pretty summer dresses, and a few men in business suits.

"They are RCMP officers and their wives and guests," Dave explained to Tammy. "The man in the straw hat is the mayor of Regina. He will take the salute this afternoon."

The band began to play "The Maple Leaf Forever". The Musical Ride rode out onto the field. The inspector rode first, followed by the eight rows of horses and riders, four abreast.

They all looked even more splendid now. In the sunshine the horses seemed to be covered in shiny black silk. The riders sat as straight as toy mounties, and their scarlet tunics glowed like fire. The inspector had a sword in a leather holder hanging from his saddle. All the other mounties held their long lances upright, the red and white pennons fluttering in the breeze. The horses held their heads high and pranced to the music. Everyone in the grandstand began to clap. Tammy felt goose-bumps on her arms.

People were still clapping as the Ride reached the centre section of the stands. The mayor stood up, and so did the people near him. The inspector saluted the mayor by holding his sword upright before his face. The mayor raised his hat. The Ride moved on, and everyone sat down.

At the end of the field, the Ride turned and halted. The inspector rode back to the grandstand, saluted again, and asked the mayor if he might begin the performance. The mayor agreed. The inspector rode back to the end of the field, then off to one side. The band began to play "Vive la Canadienne". The thirty-two horses began to trot.

Suddenly Tammy felt glad that she had worn her best dress instead of her usual slacks.

For almost half an hour she watched the horses trot and canter through one movement after another. When they stopped for a rest half-way through, she saw the riders do lance drill.

Her father told her the name of each figure as the sleek black horses formed The X, The Diamond, The Clover Leaf, the Wagon Wheel, and so on. When they trotted into The Maze, Tammy was surprised that they found their way out. When they did Threading the Needle, with one line of horses crossing through the other line, she was amazed that they didn't bump into one another. She was always surprised that as soon as the music changed, the horses changed their step and began to form a different pattern.

"The Ride horses certainly are clever," Tammy said. "Blackie will grow up to be that kind of horse."

"Forget about Blackie and watch The Charge," Dave said.

The horses by now had lined up at one end of the field. They stamped and fretted as if they could hardly wait. Their riders lifted their lances out of the little leather buckets fastened to their right stirrups. They pointed their lances straight ahead, and looked as if they. too, were waiting for something.

A trumpet call rang out. The Charge! Suddenly the horses set off at a full gallop to the other end of the field. Their riders leaned forward, shouting and urging them on, faster and faster. The moment they reached the other end, the black horses and their scarlet-tunicked riders stopped as suddenly as they had started.

The crowd in the grandstand clapped and cheered. Tammy clapped and cheered as loud as anyone.

Quickly the mounties put their lances back in the leather buckets. They reined their horses around to face the opposite end of the field.

Another trumpet call rang out. The Rally! This time there was no burst of speed. The horses cantered back to where they had begun The Charge. There they wheeled around and formed the same eight rows of four in which they had marched onto the field.

The inspector rode from the side of the field to the head of the Ride. The band began to play the RCMP "Regimental March".

The Ride marched past Tammy's section of the grandstand. The mayor and the people near him stood up. The inspector saluted him with his sword, and the mayor raised his hat.

Hardly knowing what she was doing, Tammy sat up very straight and gave a little bow.

The crowd kept clapping and cheering while the Ride marched off the field. The horses, still excited from The Charge, seemed more excited by the applause. They pranced and danced till they disappeared from sight behind the grandstand.

The Browns and the Hansons and the thousands of other people began to leave the stands. To Tammy's surprise, she found herself wishing that Blackie could be a Musical Ride horse.

Chapter 7

Blackie Becomes Burmese

When the Browns got back to Fort Walsh, Tammy told Scottie all about the Musical Ride. She kept talking about how big the horses were.

"Now you know I was right about Blackie being too small," Scottie said.

Tammy nodded. "But when I saw the Ride, I began wishing she'd grow big enough to be in it some day."

"She'll have to grow a mighty lot before the inspection committee comes this fall," Scottie said.

"I know." Tammy's voice shook.

"Anyway," Scottie said, "I thought you wanted her to stay small so you could keep her."

"Maybe I do, and maybe I don't," Tammy said. She walked away in case Scottie began teasing her.

The trouble was, she didn't know what she really wanted. Whenever she was with Blackie, she wished the loveable foal would stay small. But when she thought the Musical Ride, with everybody clapping and cheering, she hoped Blackie would some day become a Ride horse. The only thing she knew for sure was that she hoped the mounties would keep using horses. Then her father would keep his job.

During September, Tammy settled into Grade 6. But even in school she often thought of Blackie. The filly was growing, but not enough to catch up with the other foals. The girl still didn't know what to wish about her.

By the middle of October, fall was well along at Fort Walsh. The leaves had fallen from the poplar trees. The days were bright but cool. The nights grew so cold that everyone knew the ground would soon freeze. There was scarcely any grass left in the summer pasture, and new grass would not grow till spring. The horses were growing their rough winter coats.

Dave and Scottie moved the horses to the side hill pasture for the daytime, then took them to the feeding corral to eat and to stay overnight.

It was too cold for Tammy to teach Blackie out in the pasture. Instead, the girl visited her in the feeding corral, in early morning, late afternoon, and before she went to bed.

The foal still came to meet her. She was bigger and stronger, but she hadn't caught up with the other foals. She had more teeth and could eat pieces of apple and even cube sugar. When Tammy was ready to leave the corral, Blackie always followed her, nudging the girl with her nose and nuzzling her tidbit pocket. often she lifted her left front foot as if asking for one more treat.

The only time Blackie paid no attention to Tammy was while she was being weaned from her mother. The foals were about six months old then, and could eat grass and chopped oats. They no longer needed their mothers' milk.

One day the men put the foals in a small corral, while the mares stayed in the feeding corral. The foals began neighing for their mothers, and the mares neighed back. The noise grew louder and louder. When Tammy went to the small corral to comfort Blackie, the foal took no notice of her. She just paced back and forth, then poked her nose through the fence rails, and neighed to Minx.

It was about a week before the mares and foals stopped calling back and forth. The men let the foals go back to their mothers. Most of the mares had stopped giving milk, and the others wouldn't let the foals suckle. At last everything was quiet again at Fort Walsh. Tammy and Blackie carried on as usual.

In the middle of November, the inspection committee visited the ranch to check the horses.

Tammy knew when they were coming. She knew there would be four men: Inspector Collins, another mountie from Regina, and two men from the Department of Agriculture. She knew, too, that the four men would recommend to the commissioner getting rid of any horses that were too old, or lame, or not suited for the breeding program.

What about Blackie? Waiting to find out made that day at school the longest day in Tammy's whole life.

By the time she got home, the inspection committee had left. Her parents were in the kitchen, having a cup of tea and talking things over.

"What about Blackie?" Tammy almost shouted the moment she opened the door.

"Calm down," her father said. "The inspection committee is going to tell the commissioner that Blackie is perfect for the mounties, except that she is too small. It will recommend keeping her for another year to give her a chance to grow."

Tammy felt so happy she was afraid she might cry. She ran over and hugged her father, then her mother.

Suddenly she thought of something else. "If they say we should keep Blackie another year," she said, "that means the mounties are going to keep on using horses, doesn't it, daddy?"

"I'm afraid not," Dave replied. "Inspector Collins says he's still hearing rumours that we'll have to get rid of them. The trouble is, it's not the mounties who will decide. It's the federal government."

"Anyway," Tammy said, "we're going to keep Blackie for another year."

"We'll have to wait and see if the commissioner agrees with the inspection committee," her father said.

"I know," Tammy nodded. But she felt sure the commissioner would want to keep the special foal.

One afternoon a few weeks later, she came home from school to find her parents talking about a letter from Inspector Collins. Her father let her read the part he had marked in blue pencil. She read it aloud.

"The commissioner agrees with the inspection committee about keeping the foal of the mare Minx until the next meeting of the committee. Then its use to the Force will be considered again. The foal has been given Regimental No. 484, and the name of..." Tammy caught her breath. "...Burmese."

"Burmese!" she gasped. "What a stupid name to give a horse, especially a filly."

"Really stupid," her mother agreed.

"Anyway," Dave said, "we have to do whatever the commissioner tells us to do."

"I suppose we'll get used to calling her Burmese," Susan said.

"I won't!" Tammy declared. "To me she'll always be Blackie!"

Chapter 8
Snow Storm

Winter was always difficult at Fort Walsh. But Tammy had never known a winter as difficult as Blackie's first one. In the coldest weather, the filly's breath froze about her face, ice formed around her eyes, and icicles hung from her nostrils.

Scottie used to say that the only thing that didn't freeze solid at Fort Walsh was Battle Creek. He often had to break ice at the edge to let the horses drink, although the swift water in the middle channel never froze.

The worst day of Blackie's first winter came about the middle of February, although it was not unusually cold. Early that morning, the radio warned everyone about a twenty-four hour snow storm. Tammy stayed home from school, and the men kept the horses in the feeding corral.

Great snowflakes settled wherever they fell, even on the horses' backs. By late afternoon, almost twenty-five centimetres of snow had fallen. When the men went to feed the horses, Tammy went with them.

She saw the horses huddled in a corner of the corral, trying to shelter under a small group of pine trees. Blackie had a fifteen centimetre blanket of snow on her back. The girl used her mittened hand to brush it away. But by the time she had to go back to the house with the men, Blackie was carrying the first layer of another snow blanket.

At bedtime, the big flakes were still falling. The men went out again. Tammy plodded after them through the deep snow and into the dark night.

The men swung their lanterns among the horses, and Tammy used her flashlight to find Blackie. Again the girl brushed away the filly's thick blanket of snow. Again another began to build up. But again Tammy had to leave her and go back to the house with the men.

Susan had hot chocolate waiting for them. "Are the horses safe?" she asked.

"Quite safe," Dave answered.

"But they all have a lot of heavy snow on their backs," Tammy said. "Daddy, why don't you and Scottie clean the snow off them?"

"The horses will be fine as long as the weather stays cold," Dave said. "The only danger will be if the weather warms up enough to melt their snow blankets. It would be very bad for them if it froze again before they dried off."

"Many years go," Scottie said, "some horses and cattle froze to death that way."

"Don't worry, Tammy," her mother said. "As long as we keep the horses in the corral, the men can dry them off if they need to."

Tammy did worry, though, especially after she went to bed. As soon as she fell asleep. she dreamed she saw Blackie coated with ice. She woke up and ran to the window. It was still snowing! Blackie had not turned into an ice statue! Tammy got back into bed and went to sleep again. There stood Blackie again, frozen to solid ice.

Tammy couldn't bear it. She crept out of bed, put on her warmest clothes, and took her flashlight from the bedside table. She tiptoed to the kitchen, put on her snow boots, parka and mittens. Quietly she opened the door and went out into the snowy night.

Everything was quiet and dark. The only thing she could see in the light of her flashlight was the falling snow. The tracks she and the men had made earlier were filled with snow. But she had to get to Blackie. She started pushing through the deep snow, aiming for the feeding corral.

The girl felt strange being out alone in the storm-dark quiet of the night. She couldn't hear a sound except the swishing of her legs pushing through the knee-deep smow.

After a while, she thought surely she should have reached the corral. But wherever she pointed her flashlight, there was neither fence nor gate. She felt as if she had waded through heavy snow forever. And still no corral!

Suddenly she felt she was lost. She'd read stories of people getting lost in snow storms. They couldn't see, and went round and round in circles. If nobody saved them, they froze to death.

Tammy knew she hadn't been going in a straight line, or she would have reached the corral by now. Her heart began to pound with fear. Nobody knew she was out! She could freeze to death before anybody missed her! She had better follow her tracks back to the house, and tend to Blackie in the morning.

She turned around. Her flashlight showed her the track she had just made. She took a few steps back along the track she had made through the deep snow. How much easier it was backtracking! She'd soon be home, and safe.

Then she thought of Blackie the ice statue. Her legs refused to keep moving. She told herself it wasn't warm enough to thaw the snow, so Blackie wasn't in danger. But what if Blackie's snow blanket was so heavy that she'd have to lie down? She might not be able to get up!

Tammy knew she had to find out if Blackie needed her.

She turned around, and started plodding again through the deep snow. She felt she couldn't push one step farther. Then she had an idea.

"Blackie! Where are you?" she shouted. "Answer me!"

Whether or not Blackie answered, Tammy couldn't tell. But she heard a horse snort. Then another horse, and another. But the sounds were not coming from the direction she was walking! They were coming from far off to one side! If she hadn't heard the horses, she would never have found the corral!

She felt weak at the knees. She might have wandered into the creek. Then she would have become an ice statue. But now she was safe! Safe! Safe!

She followed the horse sounds to the corral, and climbed over the fence. She knew the horses would be standing in tight groups against the storm and the cold. She would have a hard time pushing through them. They might crush her or step on her.

"Blackie!" she called. "Come, Blackie!"

The filly didn't come. Tammy had to go and find her. She moved into the nearest group of big black animals that towered above her. She talked to them as she had heard her father talk.

Maybe the heavy snow and the cold made the horses less exciteable than usual. Now they had even bigger snow blankets than before. They moved apart to make way for the girl who shone her flashlight among them. Luckily, none of them kicked, but some snorted. At each snort, Tammy gave a little shiver of fear.

She eased her way into another tight group of horses, and kept calling Blackie's name. At last a soft little whinney of welcome answered.

A moment later, the flashlight shone on Blackie and her new blanket of gleaming snow. The filly whinnied again. But she was so hemmed in by bigger horses that she could only lift her head and stretch her nose toward Tammy. The other horses seemd to know that Tammy was a friend. They moved aside to let her pass.

The girl threw her arms about the filly's neck. Blackie turned her head to nuzzle her as best she could. The two stood there while the other horses stared at them in the light of Tammy's flashlight. Then the girl pushed the snow blanket from the filly's back.

"You'll be all right till morning," Tammy said, patting the filly. "Now I have to go, or my tracks will be covered with snow."

Tammy made her way back through the horses. The snow was still falling, but not so heavily. It had not hidden her track. With the aid of her flashlight, she soon found it. She had no trouble following it back to the fence, and then, by a round-about way, back to the house. She tiptoed to her room and crept into bed.

Early next morning the storm ended. The horses began moving about, and most of the show fell off their backs. By the time Dave and Scottie saw them, Blackie's snow looked no different from the others'. The men didn't guess what had happened. A little later, a snow plow cleared the road, and a very sleepy Tammy went to school.

Another Chance To Grow

Susan Brown said that Tammy's twelfth birthday, on March 21, was her happiest sign of spring. There were other signs, too, of course. The sunshine felt warmer. The snow began to melt. The leaf buds on the poplar trees began to fill out. The horses would soon begin to shed their winter coats.

A week or so after Tammy's birthday, another sure sign of spring came to Fort Walsh. Two mounties from Regina arrived in the big RCMP truck, bringing a stallion for the breeding season. When they went back, they took two of the three-year-olds to the police stable. There the horses would be trained as equitation horses. Then they would be used to help recruits – young mounties in training – learn to ride. Later, the best of the blacks would be promoted to the Musical Ride when there was need of them.

A few days after the mounties' first trip, they returned with another stallion. They took back two more of the three-year-olds. They came again till they had taken all of them, 27 that year.

The truck always left early in the morning. Tammy often saw the mounties loading the three-year-olds before she went to school. Each time she wondered if Blackie would ever grow big enough to go to Regina.

First, though, the filly had to grow big enough by fall for the mounties to keep her. Even that wouldn't do any good if they stopped using horses.

"Nobody knows what will happen," her father told her. "Keep enjoying Blackie while you can."

Tammy did just that, but things were different now Blackie was one year old. She joined the other yearlings, galloping about and splashing through the creek.

Even so, Blackie was always happy to see Tammy. The filly didn't seem to mind being tied to a tree. She stood quite still while Tammy brushed her or combed her mane and forelock. She still let Tammy lead her, and lift her feet in exchange for tidbits. She didn't need either Minx or Tammy the way she used to. The girl now had more time to visit her school friends who lived on nearby ranches.

The main difference this year was Blackie's size. When Inspector Collins visited the ranch in the summer, he was pleasantly surprised. Tammy had ridden to the pasture with him and her father. She called Blackie, then led her to the men so that the inspector could have a good look at her. When the filly held up her head, her chin was level with the top of Tammy's head.

"She's grown a lot," Inspector Collins said. "She's fleshed out well, too, and she seems strong and sturdy. And she's still as gentle and as lovely as ever."

"She'd make a perfect horse for the Musical Ride, inspector," Tammy said.

The inspector looked puzzled. "I thought you wanted your father to buy her," he said.

"Not any more," Tammy said. "Ever since we saw the Ride last summer, I want her to be in it."

"I warned her not to pester you, sir" Dave broke in. "She knows we have to wait for the inspection committee this fall before we even know if we're keeping Burmese."

The inspector nodded. "We must remember, too," he said, "that although she's a splendid animal, she's still much smaller than the other yearlings."

Remember it? Tammy always remembered it, all the rest of the summer and into the fall. She remembered it especially on the day she knew the inspection committee would visit Fort Walsh.

"What's the news about Blackie?" she asked the moment she got home from school.

"It's good news," her mother smiled. "Calm down and listen."

It was indeed good news. The committee could see that Burmese was growing to be an unusually fine filly. They didn't want the RCMP to lose her just because she was still too small. They recommended something the mounties had never done with a young horse.

Instead of Burmese staying at the ranch until she was three years old, the committee thought she should go to Regina when she was only two. There she would live in the stable, and have the best possible food, exercise, and grooming. They hoped that by the time she was three, she would have grown as big as the three-year-olds that had lived outdoors at the ranch.

In mid-December, Dave had a letter from Inspector Collins.

"The commissioner agrees with the inspection committee about Regimental No. 484, Burmese," the letter said. "Next spring, when the truck takes the three-year-olds to Regina, it will also take the two-year-old Burmese."

Then came another surprise. Burmese's half-brother, Beau, would go with her, and would have the same treatment. The commissioner wanted to find out if a normal sized two-year-old would benefit from the special treatment.

The next spring, a few weeks after Tammy's thirteenth birthday, she came home from school one day and saw the mounties' horse truck parked in the ranch yard. She knew that soon it would take Blackie and Beau to Regina.

Two weeks later, the mounties took the last of the three-year-olds. Then they came for Burmese and Beau.

Next morning before breakfast, Tammy went as usual to the feeding corral. She gave Blackie half an apple and a lump of sugar. The filly followed her to the gate, nuzzling Tammy's tidbit pocket and nudging her side.

At the gate the filly gave the girl another nudge, then lifted her left front foot. Tammy gave her the other half of the apple. When Blackie leaned down for it, Tammy threw her arms around her neck. Then she hurried away without looking back.

After breakfast, she went out with her parents and Scottie to watch the mounties load the two young horses. First they led the gentle filly, then the livelier colt, up the ramp and into the back of the truck. Tammy looked as if she might cry.

"Why don't you go and say another goodbye to Blackie before the men put up the tail gate?" her father said quietly.

Tammy walked up the ramp and into the truck. The young horses' halter ropes were tied to iron rings fastened to the cab of the truck, but they could turn their heads enough to see who was coming. Blackie gave a low whinney of welcome. Tammy patted her neck and stroked her face. Then she hurried back down the ramp.

A few minutes later, the three Browns and Scottie stood watching the truck leave. It made its way over the valley floor and along the winding trail up the far side hill. Then Dave and Scottie went to attend to the horses. Tammy and her mother watched the truck till it reached the flatland at the top and moved out of sight. Tammy felt even closer to crying.

"Don't fret," her mother said, putting her arm around her daughter's shoulders. "The mounties will take good care of her."

"I know, mom." Tammy's voice shook. "I'm glad that now she won't be out in thunder storms and snow storms. And she'll have a chance to grow and get into the Musical Ride. Just the same, I'll miss her."

"Of course you will." Her mother's arm gave her shoulders a gentle squeeze. "But you're a teen-ager now, grown up enough to go into Grade 8 this fall. And next year you'll be at Maple Creek taking your first year of highschool. That will be more fun than going to our little one-room school at Meadowlands. In Grade 9 at Maple Creek there'll be more than twenty girls and boys your age. You'll have lots of chances to make friends."

"I know, mom," Tammy agreed. "I'm glad I'm growing up, and I'm glad I'll be in highschool next year. And I know I'll make friends at Maple Creek. But I'll still miss Blackie."

"Of course you will," her mother said again. "I can imagine just how you feel."

But as they walked to the ranch house, Tammy knew that even her mother couldn't imagine how much she would miss her beautiful, clever, loveable Blackie.

Part Two

Pride of the Mounties

Chapter 10
With The Mounties At Regina

In the late afternoon, the truck reached the RCMP barracks at Regina. It backed up to the wire gate of a small pasture behind the buildings. The mounties let the young horses loose in the pasture.

At first they stood still, looking about them. Everything was different from Fort Walsh. There were no hills, no trees, only endless, flat, treeless prairie. The ground was hard, with only a few sproutings of tough prairie grass. No creek ran through the pasture. Any thirsty horse must drink from the metal trough. The fence was not made of pine or poplar rails, but of wide-mesh Page wire.

The large brick buildings looked strange. Strangest of all, there were no horses in sight: they were all in the stable.

Nothing reminded Burmese and Beau of home. They heard strange sounds: men shouting, men marching, bugles blowing. When a mountie took them some hay, they found it was dry, and had a lot of scratchy weeds in it. The water from the metal trough didn't taste right, either.

That night they found no place to shelter from the cold prairie wind, no other horses for company. Burmese and Beau lay down close together, by the water trough. A mountie night guard came every few hours, and shone a flashlight on them. By the time they got up, hoping for company, he had gone.

In the middle of the night, not far from the barracks, the CPR transcontinental train flashed and clattered and whistled past. The young horses galloped frantically round and round their small enclosure, looking for a way out. By the time they had settled down again on the hard cold ground, back came the night guard with his flashlight.

Morning was more pleasant. Bright sunshine warmed them. The sound of bugles and of men marching were not so strange now. When a freight train clattered past, the filly and the colt just pricked up their ears and watched it. Best of all, they saw a lot of horses being ridden from the stable out to the open prairie.

About mid-morning, two men walked to the pasture fence, their spurs jingling. The one in blue uniform was the commanding officer. The other, in blue breeches, brown jacket and Stetson hat, was the riding master. He was also the one Tammy knew as "another mountie from Regina" on the inspection committee.

Burmese walked up to the men and put her nose against the fence. She looked as if she wanted to make friends. Beau stayed where he was.

The riding master stroked her neck. "You see, sir," he said, "Burmese is everything I said she was, pure black, with good conformation, and good-natured."

The commanding officer looked thoughtful. "I do see, Staff," he said. "But she's even smaller than I expected. Anyway, what are you going to do with these two young horses?"

"They'll go in the two big box stalls, sir," the riding master replied. "They'll have three meals a day and bran mash on Saturday. Every day they'll have good grooming, exercise, and fresh air out in the pasture. The recruits can do the work, but I'll put Corporal Anderson in charge of them. He'll make sure that only the best recruits handle them."

"A corporal of her own, no less!" the commanding officer chuckled.

From the moment Corporal Andy led Burmese to the box stall in the big stable, she enjoyed life with the mounties at Regina. She could walk about freely in the big box stall. She could look through the steel bars along the top of the front. She couldn't see Beau in the next box stall, but she often whinnied to him. Beau always whinnied back. She soon learned to press her nose into her drinking fountain, and get a drink as often as she liked.

The corporal was a riding instructor. His work was to help train the three-year-olds, and also the young mountie recruits learning to ride. He didn't have much time to spend with the little filly, so he hoped she would make friends with the other mounties.

She certainly did. She made friends with the recruits who fed and groomed her, and cleaned out her stall. When other recruits went to see "the runt from the ranch", she made friends with them, too. Members of the Musical Ride called her "our little black beauty". They all knew why she was there, and they hoped she would grow.

One of the recruits who looked after her began taking tidbits in his jacket pocket. One morning Burmese followed him to the door of the box stall. She nudged him with her nose, and nuzzled his tidbit pocket.

When he paid no attention, she lifted her left front foot. The recruit checked it, but couldn't see anything wrong. The next morning the same thing happened. And the next.

The recruit hurried to Corporal Andy.

"Burmese has hurt her foot, corporal," he exclaimed. "But I can't see what's wrong with it."

Neither could Corporal Andy, not the riding master, nor anyone else.

Burmese enjoyed the extra attention, and kept lifting her foot. When nobody gave her a tidbit, she stopped lifting it. Then everybody thought her foot had got better by itself.

After that, Corporal Andy wanted to make sure there was nothing wrong with any of her feet. He lifted each foot in turn with no difficulty. He had no way of knowing what Tammy had taught her, so he thought she was very clever.

During the first few days Burmese was in Regina with the mounties, he had helped her get to know her new home. He had led her to several places in the stable, and also outdoors. When she saw the other horses, she whinnied at them.

When he led her past the blacksmith shop, the black filly made friends with the blacksmith and his big white cat. She stood at the door watching the sparks fly as the blacksmith hammered out a white-hot horseshoe. She always nuzzled the cat sitting just inside the doorway. The cat sometimes followed her back to her box stall.

After Burmese had lived in the stable for a few weeks, Corporal Andy began taking her to the riding school. It was a large area in the same building as the stable.

The first time he took her, she was the only horse there, and he let her run free. Kicking up the tanbark spread over the floor, she ran back and forth until she was tired of running. Just then she caught sight of herself in one of the big mirrors set in the walls. They had been placed there so that the mounties could make sure they rode the way they should.

Burmese whinnied at the horse in the mirror. When it didn't whinny back, she tried to make friends with it. At last she gave up and trotted back to the corporal.

Soon he took her to the riding school when other horses were there. He let her stand and watch the instructors training the three-year-olds. Later he put a special halter on the sleek little filly, and snapped a seven metre lunge line on it. Then he held the line and let her walk or run around him in large circles.

Sometimes he had to take one of the horses for a ride on the prairie – hacking, he called it. Then he took Burmese on a short lead rope and let her walk or trot beside him.

She seemed to enjoy life with the mounties. She always whinnied a welcome to Corporal Andy. She also whinnied to any recruit who came to feed and groom her and to clean out her stall. When she and Beau were out in the small pasture, she whinnied at the mounties and their horses trotting past to exercise on the open prairie.

Just before Thanksgiving, Dave Brown went to Regina to see Inspector Collins. Before he left, the inspector took him to see Burmese and Beau. After looking at Beau, they went into Burmese's stall. Dave wasn't surprised that the filly was as friendly as ever. But he was amazed at the change in her.

"She's been here less than five months, but she's so much taller and heavier!" he exclaimed. "Although she's fine-boned, she's well-fleshed, and she looks much stronger, too."

"She's all that," the inspector said. "And as you see, she's sleek from all the grooming and good food she's had. This beautiful filly is the pet of the stable."

When Dave got back to Fort Walsh, he could hardly wait to tell Tammy, Susan and Scottie about Burmese. There were questions and answers, and then fond comments, especially from Tammy.

"I still miss her," Tammy said. "I wish I could see her again."

"Your father and I know you do," her mother said. "He is helping to arrange something for the Christmas holidays so that you'll have your wish."

As Dave told Tammy, she wondered how she could wait so long. The students of Meadowlands school would spend two days in Regina during the holiday week. A few parents would go with them, and take them to such places as the legislative buildings and the Regina museum.

The morning of the day they came home, the other girls and boys would visit the RCMP museum at the mounties' barracks. Because Tammy had visited that museum before, she could go to see Burmese instead.

"I hope the wee filly still knows you," Scottie said.

"Of course she'll know me!" Tammy tossed her head.

That night, as she sat doing her Grade 8 homework, she wasn't so sure. What if Blackie didn't remember her? Don't be silly, she told herself. Of course she'll remember me. But what if she doesn't? She will, she will! But maybe she won't . . .

Oh, why did Scottie tease her the way he did?

There was only one thing Tammy knew for sure. If Blackie didn't remember her, she'd never let Scottie know. Never!

Chapter 11

Tammy Visits Burmese

The bitter wind cold didn't spoil that Christmas holiday trip. Tammy wore her new green parka and brown slacks, and didn't even feel the minus thirty degrees cold. Everything was super: the bus trip to Regina, staying in a motel, and visiting places of interest in the city. Then at last, the morning of the day the Meadowlands students would go home, Tammy went to visit Burmese.

Feeling excited, she walked from the museum, where the bus stopped, to the big brick stable.

There at the door, just as her father had promised, stood a tall mountie in breeches and boots, brown jacket, and fur cap.

"I'm Corporal Anderson, better known as Andy," he smiled. "I suppose you're Tammy, and you've come to visit Burmese."

"That's right, Corporal Andy," she said.

They stepped inside the big door. Corporal Andy pointed out anything of interest as they walked along the brick-paved walk-ways.

First there was the Musical Ride tack room, with rows of lances, saddles and bridles. There were also a lot of silver trays and shields, all "thank you" gifts to the Ride.

Before Tammy could ask about Blackie getting into the Ride, about twenty horses came in through the big back door. Each horse was led by a young man wearing a buffalo coat, blue breeches, a fur cap, and moccasins. The horses, mostly black but some brown, had frost on their faces, and icicles hanging from their nostrils. They clattered noisily along the brick paving.

"The young men are recruits," Corporal Andy explained. "They have been exercising the equitation horses out on the prairie."

The young mounties led the horses to the stalls that lined one side of the stable. Tammy followed the corporal as they walked behind the row of horses. Farther along the walk-way she saw the feed room where the mounties kept nothing but oats. Everything was so different from Fort Walsh.

At last Corporal Andy led her to two box stalls. Now she had the biggest surprise of all.

"Here we are," the corporal said. He opened the door of the end box stall, and stepped aside to let Tammy enter.

The girl just stood and stared. In the big stall, nearly as big as the Browns' living room, stood a sleek jet black filly. She stood munching contentedly at her manger of hay, looking as if she had always lived in luxury.

Tammy gasped. "Are you sure this is Blackie?"

"I know she came from the ranch last spring, the corporal said. "And I know her name is Burmese. Look!" He pointed to the wooden name plate above the door. Big letters along the top read, "484-BURMESE-1962". A lower line read "FAUX PAS . . . MINX".

"She's Blackie, all right," Tammy said. "But she's so polished!"

She didn't have time to worry about whether Blackie would know her. As the filly heard Tammy's voice, she turned, stretched out her neck toward the girl and whinnied softly. As Tammy walked toward her, Burmese walked toward Tammy. The filly nudged the girl's side and began nuzzling at the pocket of her parka.

"She remembers me!" Tammy exclaimed. "She remembers me!"

"She certainly does." The corporal smiled. "She never does that to me."

Tammy took out the chocolate bar she had brought for the filly. She broke it in pieces and held them out one at a time. While Burmese nibbled the last bit, she looked up at the girl the way she used to do. Tammy laid her face against the filly's.

"You don't have to say good-bye yet," the corporal said gently. "We'll take Burmese to the riding school. No one is using it this morning."

He snapped a halter rope on Burmese's halter. Then he slipped a second halter over her head. They all moved out of the stall. A horse whinnied from the next box stall and Burmese answered.

"That's Beau," Corporal Andy said. "He usually comes with us."

"I'd forgotten about Beau," Tammy said. She went into the colt's stall for a few minutes.

Then she, Corporal Andy and Burmese headed for the riding school. Tammy chuckled. "I feel like a mother going to school on parents' day," she said.

While the corporal went to get the lunge line, Tammy held Burmese at the open door of the blacksmith shop. The filly whinnied at the horse being shod, and nuzzled the white cat as usual. Tammy beamed.

A few minutes later, the three of them went into the empty riding school. The corporal closed the heavy door behind them.

First he gave Tammy time to look around the big brick school room. He explained that the two and a half metre high inner walls of wood sloped in at the bottom so that the riders' legs would not be crushed if the horses went too close to the walls. He also told her what the mirrors were for. He pointed up to the glassed-in visitors' balcony at the end of one wall.

Corporal Andy removed the filly's halter rope and snapped the seven metre lunge line on her special halter. Then he led her to the centre of the school. She circled around him as if she enjoyed showing off.

When the corporal thought she had done enough, he unsnapped the lunge line and let her run free. Kicking up the tanbark from the floor, she ran to the far end of the school. Then she wheeled around and ran to Tammy's end. Back and forth, back and forth she sped. At last she galloped at top speed toward Tammy and the corporal, and came to a sudden stop. It reminded Tammy of the Musical Ride horses at the end of The Charge.

Corporal Andy waved Burmese away. Again she ran about, tossing her head. At last, at the far end of the riding school, she turned to face Tammy and the corporal. There she stood perfectly still, looking like a jet black statue.

Tammy felt a lump in her throat. "She's more beautiful than ever!" Her voice shook.

"She certainly is," Corporal Andy agreed. "What's more, I believe she's going to grow big enough for the Mounted Police."

That did it. Tammy felt her eyes brim with tears. Of course she had wanted Blackie to grow big enough for the mounties and get into the Musical Ride. But she had also dreamed of owning the lovable filly. Suddenly it seemed as if the wrong dream was going to come true. If Blackie stayed with the mounties, Tammy would have to say good-bye forever.

Scarcely knowing what she was doing, the girl began walking slowly toward Burmese. The filly walked toward her, and they met about halfway. Burmese lowered her head nearly to the ground, and held it there while Tammy stroked her forehead. The girl tried to talk to her, but instead she began to sob.

Tammy told herself that she was a teenager now, too old to cry in front of Corporal Andy. But that didn't help. She still sobbed.

The girl and the filly stayed facing each other for a few minutes. Then Tammy dried her eyes, turned around and slowly walked back to Corporal Andy. Burmese followed, her head bowed. It seemed as if the filly knew how the girl felt, and shared her sorrow.

"Don't take it so hard, Tammy," Corporal Andy comforted her. "You must come again, as often as you like."

With a great effort, Tammy managed a faint smile. "I feel silly, crying the way I did," she said. "I'd like to come again, thank you. Thank you for today, too."

"My pleasure," the corporal smiled back at her.

He snapped the short rope on the filly's halter, and handed the other end to Tammy. "You lead her back to her stall," he said.

Back in the box stall, Tammy gave the filly a farewell hug, and moved toward the door. Burmese followed, nuzzling the pocket that had held the chocolate bar. As Tammy was about to leave, the filly nudged her in the side, and lifted her left front foot.

"Oh, Blackie! You're too smart for me!" Tammy chuckled. She took out another chocolate bar, broke it in pieces, and handed them one by one to the filly. "I was keeping this to eat on my way home," she said.

"She was too smart for us a while back," Corporal Andy laughed. "Now I know she was just trying to get more tidbits when we all thought she'd hurt her foot."

Then it was time to leave. Instead of taking Tammy back past the equitation horses, the corporal led her past the riding school to the opposite side of the building. Here they walked behind a row of big black Musical Ride horses.

"They are beautiful," Tammy said. "But nearly all of them have a bit of white on their faces or their legs. Burmese is all black, so she'd look even better in the Ride."

The corporal laughed. "You may be right," he said, "but she has a long way to go first."

At the door, Tammy thanked him once more. Then she hurried to the museum, where she met her schoolmates. After lunch at the mounties' cafeteria, they boarded the bus.

On the way home, the other girls and boys began asking questions about Blackie. Tammy's pride took over. Yes! Yes! Yes! And Corporal Andy said she was a lovely little filly. She was growing big enough for the mounties. In the riding school, on a long rope, she trotted around in circles like a circus horse.

"Don't you wish you still had her at Fort Walsh?" a girl in a red parka asked.

"Not really," Tammy said, and was surprised to realize that what she said was true. "We couldn't do as much for her as the mounties can. She has her own box stall, nearly as big as our living room. She has her own drinking fountain, and Corporal Andy is her own corporal."

"No ordinary horse should be treated like that," a boy in a green jacket said.

"She's not an ordinary horse," Tammy said sharply. "She's Burmese now, and she's special." Then she leaned back and sighed contentedly.

While most of the others chattered on and on, Tammy closed her eyes and watched Burmese go through the movements of the Musical Ride. At last, the applause! The crowd couldn't seem to stop clapping and cheering. They were still clapping as Tammy nodded and dozed off.

Chapter 12

Becoming An Equitation Horse

By the time Burmese was three years old, in the spring of 1965, she had grown in several ways. She had grown twelve and a half centimetres taller, measured from the ground to the highest point of her shoulder. She was seventeen centimetres bigger in girth, the widest part around her middle. And she had gained more than 115 kilograms. She had grown big enough to become an equitation horse, and could be used to teach mountie recruits to ride.

Beau had grown, too, but not quite as much as his half-sister. He, too, would be used as an equitation horse.

So would the other seventeen "B" name horses. The horse truck brought them, two at a time, from the ranch. Their hair stood up in clumps, and their manes hung straggly and matted. By the side of Burmese and Beau, sleek and shiny, they looked like poor country cousins.

The riding master shared all nineteen "B" horses among the instructors, four or five to each. Corporal Andy kept Burmese and Beau, and had three others.

For about a week, the instructors treated the young horses from the ranch the same way they had treated Burmese and Beau. They helped them get used to being led, and the recruits groomed them. Then all the "B" horses were ready to begin learning to be equitation horses.

When Corporal Andy knew that Burmese would be used as an equitation horse, he treated her the same as the others. There were three things she didn't like. She didn't like being moved to an ordinary stall, and tied to the manger. She didn't like it when her name and forelock were clipped off, because her neck felt strange.

What bothered her most was a soft bit fastened to her halter and put in her mouth. After a while, though, she could eat tidbits and even hay without any trouble.

Then Burmese went to the blacksmith shop to be shod. She didn't mind when the blacksmith hammered the shoes on her, because the tough part of her hooves couldn't feel any pain. As she clattered back to her stall, her feet probably felt strangely heavy. But she soon got used to wearing her shoes, and lifted her feet as high as ever.

Then the three-year-olds' training began. The instructors were very patient. If a horse was slow to learn, the instructor repeated the lesson till the horse learned it.

Burmese and Beau had the same lessons as the others, beginning with the lunge line, even though they had been on it many times before. Now they learned to start and stop and to walk or trot on command.

Corporal Andy, like the other instructors, carried a long whip during the lunge lessons. Still, no instructor ever whipped a horse. He only tapped him with the bent whip sometimes, to make him pay attention. Burmese never needed to be tapped.

"This little mare is my best pupil," Corporal Andy boasted to the other instructors.

Before Burmese learned to wear a regular saddle, she wore a "stripped" saddle. It had an elastic insert in the wide strap that went around her middle. It had no stirrups or stirrup straps that would have hit against her side.

By this time, Corporal Andy had exchanged her soft bit for a hard one. Now she learned to wear reins fastened to the hard bit.

At first, the corporal used long reins, and walked behind her as if he were driving her. Soon she knew how to turn right or left when he pulled gently on one rein or the other. Then he fastened short reins to her bit, ready for when he would ride her.

First, though, she learned to wear a saddle blanket and a regular saddle with stirrups. And then, at last, she was ready to carry a rider. At this point, in mid-August, Burmese was about halfway through her training.

By then, Tammy was having her summer holidays. She was looking forward to starting high school in the fall, at Maple Creek, about fifty kilometres from Fort Walsh. She was also looking forward to Inspector Collins' summer visit to the ranch.

He arrived as usual. Before he left, he told the Browns and Scottie all about Burmese and Beau.

"Both of them are very good students," he said. "But Burmese is by far the best of all the three-year-olds."

Tammy hoped the others couldn't see that she was ready to burst with pride.

"It's a miracle your wee Blackie is doing so well," Scottie said, shaking his head.

"I'm not a bit surprised," Tammy said, tossing her head. Then she tried to think how she could get her parents to take her to Regina.

Meanwhile, Burmese's lessons went on as usual. She was now used to wearing a regular saddle and side reins fastened to her bit. She knew how to stop and start, and turn right and left. She was almost ready for Corporal Andy to ride her.

He didn't get into the saddle right away, though. First he stood at the mare's left side while another instructor held her head. Instead of putting his left foot in the stirrup, he had a leg-up from a third instructor. Then, holding the saddle, the corporal heaved himself up part-way. He leaned over it and lowered himself slowly on it. At last Burmese felt his full weight on her back.

Corporal Andy hung over the saddle, his head on one side of the mare and his boots on the other. Now the instructor at her head led her about the riding school.

Sometimes visitors in the balcony looked down and laughed.

"That mountie looks like a sack of oats on his horse's back," one of them said.

"Except for his head and legs," another man chuckled.

Corporal Andy didn't mind if people laughed at him. He knew that the way he was teaching horses was the best way. He should not sit in the saddle before his horse was used to carrying him. The horse might be frightened and try to throw him. He might get a foot caught in the stirrup and be dragged around the riding school before anyone could stop the horse. Even though Burmese was a very good-natured horse, he knew he should train her the way he trained the others.

Soon Corporal Andy sat in the saddle with his legs dangling free. Once again another instructor led Burmese around the riding school. At last the corporal knew it was safe to ride with his feet in the stirrups. He rode his favorite mare in the regular way, and guided her back and forth in the riding school, in circles and in figure-eights.

Later, Corporal Andy stayed on her back for thirty minutes at a time. All the time he was riding, he was teaching her to obey the commands he gave by voice and by the reins and his feet and legs. She obeyed him at once. She still lifted her feet daintily, and looked as if she was enjoying everything.

Burmese had learned to step over a long pole when she was on the lunge line. Now Corporal Andy added a second pole, more than a metre from the first one, and rode her over them. The young mare learned to place her feet between the poles, at a walk and at a trot. Later she learned to do the same thing with three poles, then four.

Then she learned to go over her first jump. About three metres after the fourth pole, the corporal placed a jump about thirty centimetres high. Then he rode the mare across the poles and over the jump. It was so low that she seemed to step over it. But it was a beginning, and Corporal Andy was very pleased with the good-natured black mare.

At last the remounts learned to canter. Burmese didn't have any trouble. But most of the horses had problems with that slow, controlled gallop. They couldn't make their feet touch the ground in what the instructors called a three-beat gait. Instead, they wanted to gallop freely, the way they had done at Fort Walsh. But at last all the "B" name three-year-olds were able to canter on command.

Toward the end of November, Burmese and Beau and the other seventeen remounts were ready to help train recruits to ride.

Tammy looked forward to hearing all about Burmese when the inspection committee went to the ranch at the end of that month. The last Friday afternoon in the month, her mother drove her home for the weekend. As they went through the big gate marked, "Fort Walsh – Royal Canadian Mounted Police", she saw the inspection committee had not yet left. The four men were sitting in the car, still talking to Dave.

"Inspector Collins!" Tammy shouted as she got out of the car, forgetting she was now a "cool" teenager. She ran up to him in great excitement. "How's Blackie?" she gasped.

Her father frowned at her, but the inspector smiled.

"If you mean Burmese," Inspector Collins said, "you'd better ask the riding master." He nodded toward the mountie in the driver's seat. "He knows all about her."

"Indeed I do," the riding master said. "Burmese is one of the best horses we've ever had. We don't give marks at the riding school, but if we did, I'd give that lovely young mare an A-plus."

Tammy's face lit up with pleasure. "Do you think she'll soon be ready for the Musical Ride?" she asked.

The riding master shook his head. "She needs a few years in equitation first. And then she'll have to wait till the Ride needs another horse."

Suddenly his smile faded. "By that time," he continued, "the Mounted Police will probably have stopped using horses. So don't count on Burmese ever getting into the Musical Ride."

Tammy did count on it, though. For years she'd been hearing about the mounties giving up their horses, but they still had them. Maybe they would always have horses. Why should she worry about what might never happen?

As she stood with her father, watching the men drive away, she was not the least bit worried. Of course an A-plus horse would get into the Musical Ride! All she and Blackie had to do was be patient for a few years.

Chapter 13
Helping Train Recruits

Now the riding instructors began using the "B" equitation horses to help teach the recruits to ride. For each class of twenty-four, they placed a few of the "B" horses among the older ones. This helped the young horses get used to doing the right thing.

Corporal Andy always chose Burmese for his class, because she always did the right thing.

Almost as soon as the riding classes began, so did Burmese's troubles. When recruits put her saddle blanket on the wrong way, the creases hurt her back. One recruit poked the hard toe of his left foot in her belly each time he got on her.

A recruit in Corporal Andy's class didn't tighten her saddle girth enough. When he tried to get on, the saddle slid down her side and hung upside down under her belly. The recruit fell clear. Burmese, terrified, bolted out of line and galloped round the school. The saddle bounced against her soft belly. The metal stirrups banged at her legs.

Corporal Andy urged his horse after her. He was able to catch hold of her bridle and bring her to a stop. She stood sweating and trembling as he ordered the red-faced recruit to come and remove the saddle.

"As for you," the corporal frowned at the recruit, "you're lucky you were not allowed to put your feet in the stirrups yet. You could have been dragged around the riding school. Now take that young mare back to her stall. Give her a wipe-down, and put a blanket on her. I'll talk to you later."

After a few more lessons, the recruits rode at a walk, single file, around the school. They still had to keep their feet out of the stirrups. Also, they had to keep their arms folded. They couldn't use the reins in case they pulled too hard on the horses' mouths.

Later the recruits learned to trot slowly. They still didn't use the stirrups or the reins. Even slow trotting was much harder than walking.

A recruit in Corporal Andy's class raised his hand. "What if we fall off, corporal?" he asked.

"If you fall off, you fall off!" Corporal Andy snapped. "We can't risk you men injuring the horses! Recruits are a dime a dozen, but a good horse is hard to find. Ride! Tro-o-o-t!"

No matter how hard it was for the recruits to keep their balance, they, like the horses, seemed happy to be moving faster. The few recruits who fell off simply brushed off the tan-bark, ran to catch up with their horses, and got on again. Burmese and the other horses pricked up their ears with pleasure. The riders looked in the big wall mirrors and smiled to see that they were riding the way they should, on sleek, well-groomed horses.

Even Corporal Andy seemed to be having a good time. He kept shouting:

"Keep your stomach in!"

"Keep your back straight!"

"Knees in! Heels down! Toes up!"

After the recruits had good balance and a "good seat", they were ready for jumping, but still with legs dangling and arms folded. Then Burmese had more trouble.

The recruits lined up in single file, ready to jump. The jump was the same as the horses had used earlier, only thirty centimetres high. But to a recruit they must have seemed much higher. Some recruits fell off as their horses took the jump.

One day in Corporal Andy's class, Burmese's rider lost his balance. As the mare came down from the jump, instead of leaning back, the recruit leaned forward.

He slid forward out of the saddle. His seat rested on the mare's shoulders, his body along her neck. His head rested between her ears. He threw his arms around her neck, then tightened his grip till he almost choked her.

Instead of bolting, as she had done when the saddle slipped, Burmese froze in her tracks. She stood still, trembling and waiting for help.

"Ride! Halt!" Corporal Andy shouted. He was just in time to stop the oncoming line of horses from piling up.

The corporal was almost as upset as Burmese. Again he ordered a red-faced recruit to take her to her stall for a wipe-down and a blanket.

For the next few weeks, the corporal used Burmese as his own horse.

When the recruits had improved enough to use their stirrups and reins, Corporal Andy gave Burmese to his best recruit. The mare and her rider did so well together that he soon placed them ahead of the other horses as the leading file.

As soon as the recruits could ride well, the instructors took them out on the prairie. There in the bitter cold of early February, they walked and trotted in wind and snow.

The indoor lessons went on, too. Soon the recruits began learning simple cavalry drill. They learned to walk and trot their horses in single file, in pairs, in fours, and in eights. The recruits also learned how to wheel their horses to another direction and how to turn on the spot. Burmese, still leading file, did everything the way she should.

When Dave paid his next visit to Inspector Collins, he heard the good news about Burmese. He also heard bad news.

"Things look bad for us," the inspector told him. "It's official that during the coming year, the federal government will decide whether or not we keep our horses. They have to cut expenses somehow, and it looks as if the horses will have to go."

On the way home on Friday afternoon, Dave picked up Tammy at Maple Creek, and took her home for the weekend. On the way to Fort Walsh, he told Tammy the good news about Burmese.

"I'm not surprised!" she beamed. She settled back to think about her Blackie the rest of the way home.

At supper time he told the other three the bad news. Susan and Scottie looked shocked.

"Lord help us!" Scottie said. "Within a year, no horses and no jobs!"

"We'll have to plan for the future," Susan said.

"Right!" Dave said firmly. "We'll work something out for when we have to leave the ranch."

The others were surprised that Tammy didn't look upset.

"I don't believe it," she said, tossing her head. "For years people have been saying the mounties would have to give up their horses, but it didn't happen. I don't believe it will happen now!"

She didn't believe it when she had her fifteenth birthday in March. She didn't believe it when Burmese had her fourth birthday in May. By the end of June, when she passed out of Grade 10, she was so used to not believing it that she was sure it would never happen.

In early July, though, during her summer holidays, she had a dreadful shock. She and her parents and Scottie were having their noon meal when they heard the news on the radio.

"The Commissioner of the Royal Canadian Mounted Police," said the voice on the radio, "has announced that the RCMP will no longer use equitation as part of recruit training. The commissioner has also announced that the RCMP will keep the Musical Ride."

"So at last we know for sure!" Dave exclaimed. "And it's not as bad as it might have been. If the mounties keep the Ride, they'll still have to breed black horses. That means they'll have to keep the ranch, and you and I will still have our jobs, Scottie."

Dave, Susan and Scottie were beaming with joy at the news. Tammy knew that she, too, should be happy. But thoughts of Blackie left no room for happiness.

All the rest of the day, and long after she went to bed that night, she kept remembering that Blackie was only an equitation horse. She would be sold, and Tammy would never see her again.

Tammy buried her head in the pillow, and tried to forget she had ever heard the heart-breaking news.

Chapter 14
A Sudden Change

The next morning, Dave had a telephone call from Inspector Collins. As soon as they had finished talking, he called Susan, Scottie and Tammy together to hear the news.

"Scottie and I can keep our jobs, but we'd all have to move to Ontario," he told them.

Susan and Scottie said they would be glad to move.

"I will, too," Tammy said. Once Burmese was sold, she wouldn't care where she lived.

Then Dave explained why they would have to move to Ontario. The Musical Ride would no longer be based at Regina. Its new home would be at "N" (Training) Division at Rockliffe, Ontario. This was near Ottawa, the capital of Canada, where the headquarters of the RCMP had been since 1920. So now the mounties would need a breeding farm not too far from Ottawa.

"It will be about a year before everything can be moved to a new place in Ontario," Dave said. He looked at Tammy. "You can still go to high school at Maple Creek till then," he told her. "When we all move east, we'll find another school for you."

Over the next few weeks, Tammy kept thinking about Burmese. She couldn't eat or sleep the way she usually did. She looked so miserable that even Scottie tried to cheer her.

"Cheer up, Tammy," her father said one day. "The equitation horses won't be sold right away. We can wait till the middle of August to go to say good-bye to Burmese. The Musical Ride will be at the Regina exhibition then, and we'll go to see it again."

Tammy thanked him, but the thought of it made her feel worse.

At the end of July, Dave went to Regina to learn more about the move to Ontario. He also went to see Burmese. The news he brought home turned Tammy's misery to joy.

"Tammy! Susan!" Dave called the moment he stepped through the kitchen door. "Come and hear the good news!"

Tammy and Susan came running.

"She's not going to be sold," Dave exclaimed. "She's in the Musical Ride!"

Tammy sank into the nearest chair. She sat staring at her father. She tried to speak, but no words came.

"It's true, Tammy," her father said. "Burmese is in the Musical Ride."

"In the Musical Ride," Tammy said slowly.

Dave explained. The Ride was in Regina, practicing for the exhibition when three of the Ride horses suddenly went lame. The riding master decided that three equitation horses should replace the lame ones. He chose Burmese, Beau, and an older horse named Walt.

"I'm not surprised," Tammy said, her eyes shining.

"It's another miracle!" Scottie said.

Even Susan and Dave thought it seemed like a miracle. Burmese was only four years old. She had been an equitation horse for less than a year. The tiny Minx foal had done as well as the big and strong Beau.

At Regina, the officer in charge of the Musical Ride trained his three new horses by placing them among the older ones. They had no trouble doing what the other horses did.

Burmese held her head high and lifted her feet as if she was enjoying herself. Her muscles rippled smoothly under her sleek black coat. Her long black tail flowed gracefully. She looked like a black statue in motion.

Tammy and her parents drove to Regina for Burmese's first performance. Before the show started, they went to see the Ride lined up behind the grandstand, just as they had done four years ago.

The riding master led the Browns to Burmese, and introduced them to her mountie.

For a moment Tammy just stood and stared. The mare's sleek coat looked blacker than ever beside her mountie's scarlet tunic. Tammy hardly believed what she saw: the white headband, the gleaming ceremonial saddle and bridle, the glistening stirrups. She saw, too, the gold MP on the blue saddle blanket, and the fuzzy maple leaf stenciled on each gently rounded rump.

"I feel as if it's all a dream," she said.

"I know how you feel," the riding master said. "When I used to see Burmese at the ranch, I didn't think she would ever get into the Ride."

"She was lucky the other horses went lame," Tammy said. "She wouldn't have wanted to be sold."

"The instructors and I didn't want it, either," the riding master said. "In fact," he lowered his voice, "we felt the same way about Beau and Walt. So we made up our minds to take out three of the oldest horses, and use the three best young ones in their place."

"You mean the three Ride horses didn't go lame?" Dave exclaimed.

"That's right," the riding master said.

"Well, bless me!" Dave shook his head.

"Burmese was even luckier than we knew," Tammy said to the riding master. "Thank you very much. Now may I stroke her?"

He nodded.

For a few moments, Tammy spoke softly to the mare as she stroked her smooth neck and face. Burmese stood quite still, as she had been taught.

"She doesn't remember me," Tammy said. She smiled as if she didn't care.

She did care, though. She cared so very much. She just wanted to hurry away without even taking out the cubes of sugar she had brought in her shoulder bag.

"Let's go and find our seats," she said to her mother. They began to walk away.

Suddenly Burmese gave a low whinny. Tammy turned for one last look. There stood Blackie with her left front foot raised.

The girl hurried back. She felt so excited that she almost trembled as she took out the sugar and held it out, one cube at a time. Her parents and the riding master smiled at one another. As Burmese nibbled each cube of sugar, she lifted her head and looked straight at Tammy. After the last one, she rubbed her velvety muzzle along the girl's arm and shoulder.

"See you next year in Ontario," Tammy murmured. She gave Burmese a farewell pat.

Later she sat with her parents and Aunt Doris and Uncle Jim in the grandstand and watched the Ride march onto the field. She could hardly believe that her dreams had come true. Yet there was her beautiful Blackie, prancing in the sunshine to the music of the mounties' band. There was her Blackie, stepping so daintily that her feet seemed scarcely to touch the ground.

Tammy beamed with pride as Blackie came out of The Maze so cleverly, and performed Threading the Needle without bumping into any other horse. And when the Ride did The Charge, it was just like one of Tammy's dreams.

At the end of the performance, just as it was at the end of the dream, came the loud applause. Even after the horses had pranced off the field, the crowd couldn't seem to stop clapping. Neither could Tammy. It made her think of her very earliest dream, on the night of the day Blackie was born. In that dream, a fuzzy, flop-eared Blackie led the Musical Ride. The queen sat on her throne, watching, and clapping.

"Tammy! Tammy!" She heard her mother's voice and felt her hand on her shoulder. Everyone was leaving!

"Wasn't Blackie wonderful!" she exclaimed as they moved toward the exit. "She'll lead the Ride someday."

"We'll have to wait and see," Dave smiled.

Tammy didn't mention the queen. Even Tammy didn't expect that part of her dream would come true.

Chapter 15
Pride Of The Mounties

In the fall of that year, the Musical Ride went to perform at towns in British Columbia. The horses travelled from place to place in big vans. They always grew very tired from having to keep their balance in the swaying vans.

At each stop Burmese used to run around at top speed each time she was let loose. At one small town she didn't notice the pasture was fenced with barbed wire, not as easy to see as the fences she knew. She ran full speed into the sharp spikes of the fence.

Two mounties saw her slam into it. She turned and galloped along it, screaming with fear. They ran after her, and one caught her by the halter.

Blood streamed down her chest and legs as he led the trembling mare to the nearest van. He used things from a first aid kit to try to stop the bleeding. The other mountie ran to a nearby house and telephoned a veterinarian.

The vet stitched up the many cuts on her chest and legs. He couldn't tell if scars would remain. The mounties knew, though, that if scars did remain, Burmese could no longer be used in the Musical Ride. She was put off duty for a week's rest. Luckily, by that time it was mid-October. There would be no more Ride performances for the rest of the year.

During the winter Burmese stayed in the Regina stable. The vet must have done a splendid job of sewing. Her wounds left no scars. She could remain in the Musical Ride!

By spring all the Ride horses had been moved to their new home, the mounties' stable at Rockliffe, Ontario.

Meanwhile, the RCMP had bought a farm at Pakenham, about fifty kilometres north-west of Ottawa. A stable had been built, big enough for all the Fort Walsh horses, and pastures and corrals were ready for them. Also, a house had been built for the Browns.

The Browns and Scottie soon enjoyed life at Pakenham, and Tammy was happy in her new school. She was also happy to be living near enough to Rockliffe to visit Burmese sometimes.

That year of 1967 was the year of Canada's hundredth birthday. The Musical Ride horses were performing away from home most of the time. They went to every province except British Columbia, where they had been the previous year.

Tammy heard all the Burmese news from her father, who heard it from an old friend. Corporal Andy had been made a sergeant and moved to Rockliffe. His job was to train the mounties who volunteered to be on the Musical Ride, so he was able to pass on all the news to Dave.

One day Tammy heard two pieces of great news. Burmese had been promoted to leading file, even though she had been in the Ride only about a year. And that fall the Ride would perform at Rockliffe! When Tammy heard the news, she was so excited that she laughed and cried at the same time. Another part of her dreams had come true!

When at last the Ride came to Rockliffe, Tammy sat with her parents in the wooden stands put up for the show. The girl beamed with pride as she saw Burmese lead Beau and the other horses through the many Ride movements. The sleek black mare pranced and danced as she had always done. When she led The Charge she galloped faster than the others and arrived first at the far end of the field.

"Burmese is the best Ride horse ever," Tammy said to her parents as they left the stands.

"I believe you're right," her father agreed.

During the following year, the Ride performed at many places in Canada, and in several cities in the United States. From Washington, D.C., the Ride traveled by air for the first time, to Bermuda and back. They flew in a huge 747 jumbo jet cargo plane.

When the Ride was at home, it performed ceremonial duties in Ottawa. Burmese helped escort the governor general to and from the opening of Parliament. He rode in a low-slung open carriage, with an escort of 32 horses and riders. Some trotted ahead, some behind. On other occasions, Burmese helped escort foreign ambassadors when they drove in a carriage to Government House.

It seemed that Burmese would lead the Ride for many years. What really happened was quite different.

In the fall of 1968, the riding master at Rockliffe, Staff Sergeant Ralph Cave had an idea. He suggested that the RCMP should offer one of their horses to Queen Elizabeth. Everybody knew that the queen loved horses. She might like to have a well-trained saddle horse to ride for pleasure. And as she was the Honourary Commissioner of the RCMP, she would probably like an RCMP horse.

"It sounds like a good idea," Commissioner M.F.A. Lindsay said. "But have we got a horse good enough for the queen?"

"Oh, yes, sir," the riding master answered. "We have the mare Burmese. She's clever, good-natured, pure black, and just the kind of horse we're trying to breed. She's only six years old, but she's the leading file of the Musical Ride. She's our very best horse."

A letter went to Buckingham Palace, asking if the queen would accept a horse from the RCMP.

"Yes, thank you," the answer came back. "Her Majesty would like a gray one."

When Tammy heard about it, she said she couldn't imagine why anyone would want a gray horse.

Another letter went to Buckingham Palace. "The RCMP have only black horses," it said. "Would Her Majesty like a black one?"

All the mounties who knew about the offer waited anxiously for the reply.

Surely the queen would say yes. She knew the mounties' black horses. Some of them had escorted her when she came to Canada and visited the Houses of Parliament. Also, she had seen some of the Musical Ride horses in 1953, the year she was crowned. They had been in the coronation procession. The next day she had invited them to visit her at Buckingham Palace. Surely, the mounties thought, the queen would like to have one of those beautiful black horses.

Tammy thought so, too. But when she knew that the mounties were planning to give Burmese to the queen, she felt torn two ways. On the one hand, it would be a great honour for Burmese to become the queen's horse. And the mare would probable have the best care and the best home in the whole world. On the other hand, once Burmese belonged to the queen and went to England, Tammy would never see her again.

Although Tammy was a young adult now, seventeen and starting Grade 12, she still felt something like the little girl she used to be. At that time, she wanted Blackie to stay small and belong to her, but also she wanted her to grow up big and get into the Musical Ride. Now she wanted

Burmese to be the queen's horse, but also she wanted the mare to stay in Canada. It was hard to be sensible about Blackie-Burmese.

Soon the queen's reply came. "Yes, thank you. Her Majesty would be pleased to accept a black horse."

A few days later, Dave told Susan, Scottie and Tammy that everything was settled. The mounties would give the queen their best horse – Burmese.

"What an honour for Burmese," Susan said.

"Another miracle!" Scottie said.

"It isn't right for the mounties to give away their best horse," Tammy said. She felt a lump in her throat. "Everybody knows the queen already has lots of good horses. I just hope she appreciates Burmese the way she should!"

"She will, Tammy," her father said gently. "Even the queen will appreciate Burmese."

Chapter 16
Tammy Says Good-Bye

As soon as Queen Elizabeth had agreed to accept a black horse, the mounties sent photographs of Burmese to her. They also sent information about her and her parents. Then Commissioner Lindsay planned when and how to send Burmese to England. He knew that the Musical Ride horses were going to fly there in late April to perform in British cities. It seemed a good idea to send Burmese with the Ride.

Officials at Buckhingham Palace agreed. Soon everything was settled. The Musical Ride was due to perform at the Royal Windsor Agricultural Show in the spring of 1969. Because Queen Elizabeth lived part of the time at Windsor Castle, Burmese could be presented to her there. The queen agreed, and set the day as Monday, April 28.

Meanwhile, the riding master ordered Burmese to be taken off the Ride. She was moved to a box stall. Once again she had her own corporal. He was Corporal Frede Rasmussen, one of the riding instructors. His job was to train the queen's horse, as everyone now called her, to be a perfect recreational saddle horse.

First the corporal made sure that Burmese remembered all that the mounties had taught her. Again and again, he guided her through the two-beat trot, the three-beat canter, and the four-beat walk. He took special care that she moved smoothly when she changed from one gait to another.

Also, the corporal often took her to special places for a different kind of training. These places had obstacles such as a horse and rider might meet in cross-country riding in England. Burmese practiced climbing up a bank of earth and jumping down the other side. She learned to jump ditches, low hedges, and piles of logs.

Ever since Tammy knew that the queen had agreed to accept a black horse, she had gone to visit Burmese almost every Saturday. The mounties were not surprised to see her. They all knew about Tammy and her pet foal that had become the mounties' best horse.

The first Saturday in April, Sergeant Andy was on weekend duty. He had just finished with the noon stable parade when Tammy arrived. He walked with her to Burmese's box stall.

"This box stall makes me think of Regina," Tammy said. "Remember when I came to visit Burmese in her big box stall when she was only two?"

"Indeed I do," the sergeant smiled.

When Tammy went into Burmese's stall, the sleek black mare whinnied a soft welcome. Sergeant Andy left them alone.

As the sergeant walked away, he remembered how sad Tammy had been when she parted from Burmese in the riding school in Regina. She must be feeling worse now, he thought. Her next parting from Burmese would be forever.

A few days later, Sergeant Andy telephoned to Dave Brown at Pakenham. He had an important message from Staff Sergeant Cave. The riding master had agreed that Tammy could ride Burmese before the mare left for England. If Tammy came to Rockliffe next Saturday afternoon, Sergeant Andy would take her hacking.

For Tammy, the rest of the school week went by like a dream. She couldn't believe what was going to happen.

After lunch on Saturday, she dressed in her riding outfit. Her parents had bought it for her when she joined the local riding club a few months ago. Carefully she put on her jodhpur-style riding breeches and her riding boots. Next came her black hunting jacket, her jockey-style hat, and her leather gloves.

Before she left her room, she checked her reflection in the mirror. Even then she wondered if the girl she saw there was really going to ride the queen's horse.

Her parents believed it, though. They drove her to Rockliffe, left her at the door of the riding school, and went off to shop in Ottawa.

As Tammy saw Sergeant Andy waiting for her, she believed it, too. She watched him saddle Burmese for her, then Beau for himself. Soon they were riding side by side, in the same open field in which Corporal Rasmussen had tested the queen's horse.

Tammy had been a good rider for many years, and she used some of the rider's aids naturally. Since joining the riding club, she had learned to use the same aids as the mounties used. She was able to signal to Burmese without any trouble.

Tammy felt happily at ease with her Blackie. The mare carried her smoothly over the level grassland and along the tree-lined riding trails. When Burmese walked, the girl felt the mare's muscles ripple. When she trotted, the two of them might well have been doing a graceful dance. When the mare cantered, Tammy felt a grandmother's rocking chair motion.

Later, back at the riding school, Sergeant Andy unsaddled Burmese before he went to unsaddle Beau. Tammy began stroking the mare with one hand, and holding out lump sugar in the other.

"I'll always remember you, my Blackie-Burmese," she whispered.

Burmese nibbled the sugar. She looked at Tammy as she had done so often over the years ever since she was a tiny foal. At last Tammy moved to the door of the box stall. Burmese followed her, nudged her, and lifted her left front foot.

"Oh, my beautiful Blackie," Tammy murmured as she held out the last lump of sugar. "Good-bye, my lovely! Good-bye!"

For a moment she held her face against the mare's. Then she hurried away without looking back.

At Beau's stall she thanked Sergeant Andy. Then, at the nearest bus stop, she caught a bus to Ottawa, where she was to meet her parents.

Back home in Pakenham, every horse, of any size, of any age, reminded her of her beloved Blackie.

Part Three

The Queen's Horse

Chapter 17

The Queen's Horse

As soon as the Musical Ride arrived in England, it performed in several cities. Burmese, meanwhile, was taken to London. She was stabled at the Knightsbridge barracks, the home of the famous Royal Household Cavalry. There she would wait until a mountie took her to Windsor Castle the day before she would be presented to the queen.

The night before she was to go to Windsor the black mare had an accident that might have caused her serious injury, or even death. A night guard making his rounds found her lying on the floor of her stall. She was struggling wildly, but not able to get up.

He could see that she had lain down too close to one wall. There was not enough room for her to stretch her front legs, so she couldn't get up the way horses always do. The night guard could see, too, from the sweat pouring from her body, that she was exhausted. But she still threw herself about, looking as if she would struggle till she died.

The night guard probably felt almost as alarmed as the mare. He was afraid that the queen's horse might be seriously injured while she was under his care. He shouted for other guards to come and help him.

Somehow they moved the dripping, trembling mare away from the wall. Now she was able to stretch her front legs and stagger to her feet.

Her own night guard dried her with towels. He put a heavy blanket on her so she wouldn't catch cold. She was still trembling when he took her out of the stall and walked her around to see if she was lame. She showed no sign of injury. But he knew that an injury might show even several hours later. For the rest of the night he visited her every half hour or so. He saw that she didn't lie down again, but she seemed to have recovered. By morning Burmese had settled down well enough to eat her hay and oats.

By the time a mountie came to take her to Windsor Castle, she was already groomed, and looked as sleek as ever. When the mountie learned about the accident, though, he in turn walked her around the stable yard. At last he felt sure that she had not been injured, and he led her into a waiting horse van. It carried them through the Sunday-quiet London streets and on to the queen's Cumberland Lodge stables at Windsor Castle.

A groom of the royal stables met them. He led Burmese to a big box stall of the kind the queen liked for her horses. As the groom explained to the mountie, Her Majesty didn't like her horses to be tied up.

The mountie told the groom about the accident at Knightsbridge barracks. The groom in turn worried that Burmese might have been injured. Once again Burmese was led outside and walked about till it seemed certain that she was sound.

"She's safe here," the groom said with relief. "Nothing can possibly happen to her now she is here in the queen's stable."

The royal groom was wrong. Burmese had a problem because the hay for the queen's horses was not put in mangers as she was used to. Instead, the hay in each box stall was held high in a net hanging from a big hook on the wall. In that way, a horse could eat it a bit at a time without spreading it about and wasting it.

At the mare's first meal, at noon, she must have found it very strange that her hay was held so high. Somehow she got the net off the hook, and it fell to the floor. She pawed the net to get at the hay, the way she pawed the snow to get at grass at Fort Walsh. Her foot caught in the net. The more she struggled to free it, the more tightly her foot was caught.

When this accident happened, though, she didn't keep struggling to free herself. Just as she had done at Regina when the recruit landed on her neck during a jumping exercise, she just stood, sweating and trembling, waiting for somebody to help her.

That somebody was the groom who came to take away the hay net. He freed her foot, wiped away the sweat, and covered her with a blanket.

On Monday morning, April 28, 1969, Commissioner Lindsay and his party stood on a lawn in front of Windsor Castle. A breeze had blown away the early morning fog, and the sun had come out.

With the scarlet-tunicked commissioner stood two other Canadian officials and the Inspector in Charge of the Ride, Inspector P.J.C. Morin, who was also wearing a scarlet tunic.

Burmese, groomed to gleaming black, and wearing her ceremonial saddlery, stood with her head held high. On her back sat Staff Sergeant Cave, his scarlet tunic aglow. Behind them stood an escort of four Musical Ride horses and their riders with lances.

Soon Queen Elizabeth walked out onto the lawn. With her were Princess Anne and their attendants. After various handshakes, Commissioner Lindsay gave a short speech. The queen thanked him for the gift of Burmese. Later she walked over to the black mare and spoke to Staff Sergeant Cave about her. Then she invited Commissioner Lindsay, the other two Canadian officials, and Inspector Morin to the castle for lunch.

While Queen Elizabeth and her guests had lunch, Princess Anne rode Burmese around the castle grounds, with the staff sergeant on another

RCMP horse. Later, while the Canadians were still with the queen, the princess joined them.

"Burmese is a very well trained horse," she told her mother. "She rides beautifully."

During lunch Queen Elizabeth asked Commissioner Lindsay if Burmese might take part in the Musical Ride at the Royal Windsor Agricultural Show in a few days.

"That might be difficult," the commissioner replied. "Burmese has been off the Ride for six months. All that time she has been trained as a recreational saddle horse. She might have forgotten the Ride movements."

Rather than disappoint the queen, though, the commissioner and Inspector Morin agreed that Burmese could perform in the Ride. But she must be placed in the body of the Ride, not in her former position as leading file.

Then Queen Elizabeth asked if Burmese's rider could carry her own pennon instead of the RCMP pennon. In that way, the queen could easily watch Burmese through the whole performance.

So Burmese performed once more, and for the last time, in the Musical Ride. Her rider, Constable John Hossfelt, carried the queen's own pennon on his lance. Thus she was able to follow the movements of her own horse among all the other gleaming blacks. When Her Majesty applauded at the end of the performance, no doubt she was thinking especially of Burmese.

"The mare," Constable Hossfelt said later, "performed as if she had never left the Ride."

When Tammy heard of Burmese's performance before Queen Elizabeth, she could hardly believe it. She thought again of her first dream of Blackie. In that dream a flop-eared foal performed with the Ride while the queen clapped in admiration.

Even in Tammy's wildest day-dreams, she had never believed that the part about the queen would come true. Yet now Blackie-Burmese had taken part in the Musical Ride at the request of the queen, and the queen had applauded her.

Suddenly Tammy no longer felt unhappy that the mounties had given away their best horse. Instead, she felt a warm glow of pride that her clever Blackie was still performing well, even as the queen's horse.

Chapter 18
The Queen's Choice

A few days after Burmese performed in the Musical Ride, Queen Elizabeth went riding on her new saddle horse. Like Princess Anne, she learned that the sleek black mare rode beautifully. She found that Burmese was well trained, and that she responded quickly to the rider's aids. The mare was quiet, good-natured and obedient. At the same time she was bright, alert and spirited. In fact, Burmese seemed like a perfect horse.

Queen Elizabeth knew she would enjoy riding her new horse for pleasure. Perhaps, she thought, she could also ride her on special occasions. The next one would be the Queen's Birthday Parade in mid-June, about six weeks away.

The Queen's Birthday Parade took place not on her real birthday, but on her official one. It was probably the most colourful state ceremony in the world. It was performed by the cavalry regiments and the Foot Guards, part of whose duties were to guard the reigning king or queen. These regiments honoured Queen Elizabeth by parading before her.

The Sovereign's Birthday Parade was first performed about two hundred years earlier, for the birthday of King George III. Queen Elizabeth's parade, like the first one, took place on the Horse Guards Parade, a large, open area not far from Buckingham Palace.

Ever since Queen Elizabeth became queen, she had ridden a handsome horse in the Royal Procession from the palace to the parade grounds. There, still mounted she reviewed the regiments that were honouring her.

Now, having ridden Burmese, the queen wanted to use her for that special occasion in June. First, though, she had to make sure that the likable black mare was as suitable as she seemed. During the procession, Burmese would have to keep calm in spite of cheering crowds, waving flags, and blaring bands. On the parade grounds she would have to stand still for long periods during the ceremony.

Queen Elizabeth made it known that she would like to ride Burmese in the coming Birthday Parade. One of her staff asked the Mounted Branch of the London Metropolitan Police to test the mare.

The Mounted Branch knew exactly what kind of horse the queen needed. In fact, for many years they had provided horses for the royal family to use in the parade. For several years Queen Elizabeth had ridden their horse, Imperial, a big chestnut. It was ready for her again this year. The trouble was, Imperial became restless when he had to stand still for a long time.

Burmese was taken from the queen's stable at Windsor Castle. Now her home would be the Mounted Branch stable at Great Scotland Yard, near the British Houses of Parliament. Then her testing began.

A London policeman often rode her to Buckingham Palace for the changing of the guard. There she saw crowds and heard loud band music, but they didn't bother her. The police thought she might be upset, as many horses were, by the high black bearskin hats worn by the guards. They didn't bother Burmese, either.

A policeman rode Burmese up and down The Mall, a beautiful avenue of trees leading from Buckingham Palace to the parade grounds. The policeman played tape recordings of bands and cheering crowds. Often he turned up the volume until it was almost painful. Still nothing bothered Burmese.

Sometimes a policeman took her to football games. Even the threatening noises of the large, unruly crowds failed to frighten Burmese.

Several times she went to the riding school of the Household Cavalry. There she had the same noise training as the Cavalry gave their own horses. Men set off small explosions to see what she would do.

A soldier's "band" marched beside her, making frightful noises. Trumpets blared and drums boomed. The "bandsmen" pounded pots and pans with pieces of metal. At the same time, other soldiers waved small flags at the black mare and shouted at her. But no matter where the police took her, and no matter what she saw or heard, Burmese was never once frightened. She just pricked up her ears, and looked at the people making the noises, as if she wondered why they were behaving that way.

The policemen of the Mounted Branch also tested her patience. This was specially important. Queen Elizabeth would often have to hold her horse's rein with only her left hand, while she saluted with her right. A restless horse might disturb the ceremony.

Now the police took Burmese on patrol. They made her stand on city streets for long periods without moving. The good-natured mare passed the time by watching whatever came along. She pricked up her ears at everything: children, grown-ups, dogs, bicycles, cars, busses, and anything else that came along.

At last everyone agreed that Burmese had passed all the tests so far. But there was another test to come. Queen Elizabeth always rode side-saddle in her Birthday Parade, and Burmese had never been ridden side-saddle. Even a well-behaved saddle horse might behave differently when carrying a rider side-saddle.

Next the police took the black mare to the queen's own riding school in the Royal Mews at Buckingham Palace. There she was ridden side-saddle by the horsewoman who always helped the queen get ready for special riding occasions. Burmese was as obedient and good-natured as usual.

"Burmese rides perfectly," the horsewoman told Queen Elizabeth. "Riding Burmese is like riding in a Rolls Royce."

When at last Queen Elizabeth went to her own riding school and rode Burmese side-saddle, she was pleased with the mare. No doubt she was also pleased that her mount for the coming Birthday Parade would not be a big, sometimes impatient police horse. She would ride her own smaller-sized, patient Burmese.

Not only the British looked forward with pleasure to the Birthday Parade of 1969. So did Staff Sergeant Cave, who was still in England with the Musical Ride. He had been invited by the queen to attend the ceremony at the Horse Guards Parade.

About that time, one of the queen's staff made a trans-Atlantic telephone call to Commissioner Lindsay. His message was that Her Majesty would ride Burmese in her Birthday Parade. So the commissioner, and also the staff at Rockliffe and Pakenham, looked forward to the event. At first Tammy, her parents and Scottie had expected to see only news clips on the CBC news. Then the CBC announced that it would televise selected parts of the Birthday Parade the following afternoon.

Tammy could hardly wait.

CHAPTER 19
The Queen's Favourite

On Sunday afternoon, Tammy, her parents, and Scottie settled themselves in front of the Brown's television to watch the CBC program of the Queen's Birthday Parade.

As the picture came into focus, they saw a long line of gleaming horses with riders in handsome uniforms. The horses, of various colours, stood perfectly still, like statues. The riders wore either scarlet tunics or blue, and either plumed helmets or black bearskin busbies. Both men and horses looked like cut-outs from a huge picture book.

"The British Broadcasting Corporation welcomes all viewers to this telecast of Her Majesty Queen Elizabeth II's Birthday Parade," a voice said. "On this sunny morning of June 14, we are in the inner courtyard of Buckingham Palace. As you can see, Her Majesty's personal mounted escort is waiting for her arrival...

"The escort is made up of officers of the Household Cavalry and of the Foot Guards, and various officials of the Royal Household. Ah! Here comes the queen's mount, Burmese. She was a gift from the Royal Canadian Mounted Police."

Tammy's face lit up as the gleaming black mare came into view, led by a royal groom in colourful livery. . She was wearing the royal ceremonial saddlery with a special bridle hung with metal chains and medallions. A royal blue saddle-cloth trimmed in gold lay on her back under a bright, highly polished side saddle with only one stirrup.

"The stirrup is of gold-gilt," the announcer said.

A few moments later a footman, also in colourful livery, placed a mounting block at the left side of Burmese. Then two men in colourful uniforms stepped forward, ready to greet the queen when she came out of the palace.

First, though, the Queen Mother and her two ladies-in-waiting came out. They stepped into a waiting carriage drawn by two gray horses, and they drove to the parade grounds. There the Queen Mother would watch the ceremony from the Horse Guards building.

Then Queen Elizabeth appeared at the King's Door of the palace. She was wearing a gold-embroidered scarlet tunic, a dark blue riding skirt, black riding boots, a small black fur hat, and white gloves.

"Her Majesty is Colonel-in-Chief of the Scots Guards," the announcer said. "That regiment will play a special part in this year's ceremony, so Her Majesty is wearing the uniform of that regiment."

As Tammy watched the queen walk toward Burmese, she saw that the mare's saddle-cloth had much more gold embroidery than the queen's tunic. She felt very proud that her Blackie-Burmese had become the queen's horse, but still a bit sad that she had lost her adorable Blackie.

"With Queen Elizabeth are Prince Philip, her husband, and the Duke of Kent, Colonel of the Scots Guards," the announcer said.

The two men, wearing scarlet tunics and black bearskin busbies, followed the queen down the steps to the courtyard.

Then Tammy saw the queen pause to pat Burmese before she prepared to mount.

Burmese stood quite still while the queen stepped onto the mounting block. Then, with the help of an official, Her Majesty stepped from the block to the side-saddle, and placed her left foot in the gold-gilt stirrup.

"Her Majesty's Canadian horse is behaving very well," the BBC announcer said. "She is standing as still as a statue."

As still as a statue! Tammy felt a lump in her throat. She was remembering the two-year-old Blackie-Burmese in the riding school at Regina, standing at the far end of the school like a jet black statue.

Now the queen was safely settled in the side-saddle. Prince Philip and the Duke of Kent mounted their horses and took their places behind the queen.

Tammy settled back to enjoy the rest of the telecast.

The queen signalled to Burmese that it was time to start. The mare held her head high as she set out at a smooth but springy walk. She carried her royal rider from the inner courtyard to the palace gate and out toward the crowds gathered there. All the waiting horsemen followed.

The moment the crowds saw the queen, they began to cheer. Wave after wave of sound struck the queen and her mount. Burmese walked on calmly.

Except for Queen Elizabeth's own group, the procession was already in place. Now she and her escort rode to their places. Ahead of them were the Life Guards. Behind were the Royal Horse Guards. Among all those big horses, Burmese was noticeably smaller, but as the queen's mount, she was the special horse of the parade.

The massed bands began to play, and the procession moved forward. Slowly it went past the Queen Victoria Memorial and along The Mall.

Thousands of people cheered, waved flags, and held children high enough to see. Camera bulbs flashed, and television cameras whirred. But Burmese was not at all disturbed.

"Her Majesty's scarlet tunic glows like fire, against her black mount," a BBC announcer said. "As many viewers know, Burmese, used to be a member of the famous Musical Ride of the Royal Canadian Mounted Police. But perhaps you don't know why the Musical Ride uses black horses....

"A Mounted Police officer thought of it after he visited London many years ago. He liked the way the black horses of the Life Guards showed off their scarlet tunics. That officer later became Commissioner S.T. Wood. Then he had the Mounted Police use black horses to show off their scarlet tunics."

Tammy and the others smiled and nodded at one another.

Although only the Life Guards wore scarlet tunics, while the Royal Horse Guards wore blue, the troopers of both regiments added greatly to the splendour of the Queen's Birthday Parade.

The metal of their helmets and breast-plates shone in the sunshine. Their polished black above-the-knee boots gleamed. The white plumes of the Life Guards and the red plumes of the others waved about with the jogging of the horses. Glistening spurs jingled, and the polished hooves of the horses clattered on the paved Mall.

Most of the time, though, the jingle and clatter were drowned by the music of the massed bands, some mounted and some on foot. The massive drum horses and the colourful livery of their riders added regimental splendour. The drum horses were specially trained large piebald horses with uneven markings of brown and white.

"The kettle drums carried by the drum horses," an announcer said, "are made of solid silver. One of them was presented to the Guards by King George III about two hundred years ago."

Yet for all the splendour of the procession, Tammy noticed that the crowds cheered loudest for the queen and Burmese.

It was the same when the procession arrived at the Horse Guards Parade Grounds at eleven o-clock exactly. People sitting in the stands seemed interested most of all in Queen Elizabeth and her gleaming mount.

Burmese kept to her smooth but springy walk as she carried the queen to the saluting base. She stood quietly while the bands played "God Save the Queen". Then the mare moved briskly while the queen rode up and down the long rows of scarlet-tunicked Foot Guards, inspecting them. Then she inspected the mounted Sovereign's Escort. All this time the massed bands played marches, some quick, some slow.

The queen returned to the saluting base. Now Burmese stood quietly during the next part of the Birthday Parade, the most important and the longest part. This was the Trooping of the Colour by the Scots Guards.

First a group from that regiment escorted their own special flag, or Colour, past long rows of Scots and other Foot Guards. Meanwhile, bands played and marched back and forth and round about. Pipers played Scottish airs on bagpipes, and drummers twirled drumsticks high above their heads. At last the Scots Guards marched past the queen, followed by the other Foot Guards on parade. Next the Household Cavalry and their mounted bands rode past, with bobbing plumes, jingling spurs, and rattling kettle drums.

Now Burmese stood still while the queen saluted the Colours of each regiment as it marched past.

"Poor Burmese must be tired of standing still," Tammy said.

Each time the television cameras focused on the saluting base, though, she could see that the black mare didn't look tired. She just kept her ears pricked forward and watched everybody and everything.

At last the ceremony at the parade ground ended, and the Royal Procession returned to Buckingham Palace.

On arriving at the palace, the queen rode Burmese to the centre gate. There she wheeled her obedient mount around, to be in place for the final march past. This time it was led by the Foot Guards who would take over guard duty at the palace.

When all the regiments had passed, Queen Elizabeth turned Burmese around once more. The black mare carried her royal rider through the palace gate, to the inner courtyard, and out of sight.

"This ends our telecast of the Queen's Birthday Parade," an announcer said. "Viewers might like to know," he went on, "that the royal grooms will now give Burmese a rub-down and a well-deserved feed of hay and oats. Later she will be vanned back to Her Majesty's Cumberland Lodge stables at Windsor Castle. There she will be ready for whenever Her Majesty next chooses to ride her favorite horse."

Tammy switched off the television. No other program was important that afternoon.

"Whoever could have guessed it!" Dave Brown exclaimed. "The under-sized foal born at Fort Walsh has become Queen Elizabeth's favourite mount."

"The wee one has surprised me again," Scottie said.

"Our Burmese has gone from prairie to palace," Susan smiled. "It's just like a fairy story."

"Oh, yes!" Tammy's voice was soft, and her eyes had a far-away look. "And it's only fair that the number one horse in the world is the queen's favourite."

Epilogue

Over the following years, Queen Elizabeth continued to ride Burmese in her Birthday Parades. She also rode her for pleasure.

The black mare spent most of her time at Windsor Castle. A few weeks before each Birthday Parade she was taken to London. There the Mounted Branch of the London Metropolitan Police made sure that she again became used to crowds and noises.

Burmese had her eleventh birthday in 1973, the year the RCMP had its hundredth birthday. Queen Elizabeth visited Canada to take part in the mounties' centennial celebrations. It seemed a good time for the RCMP to present her with another, younger black horse. The mounties changed his name to Centennial, and the queen later changed the spelling to Centenial.

The Mounted Police expected that Queen Elizabeth would use Centenial in her Birthday Parade as Burmese grew older. But the queen kept on using her favourite horse.

For the first twelve years in which Burmese acted as the queen's mount in her Birthday Parade, everything went smoothly. Then in 1981, something happened that could have caused the queen serious injury if she had been riding a nervous horse.

As Queen Elizabeth rode into the parade ground, a man in the crowd fired several blank revolver shots at close range. It was natural for Burmese to be startled. She didn't swerve, but she sprang forward a few steps. She was trying to get out of the way of the Sovereign's Escort coming up close behind her.

The queen remained firmly seated in her side-saddle, with her left foot still placed in the gold-gilt stirrup. In a few seconds she was in full control. The police arrested the man with the revolver. The queen and Burmese walked on as if nothing had happened. Later, the press, the people who had been watching on television, and the royal family, all praised the mare's behaviour.

As the years passed, Burmese needed more exercise than she was getting at Windsor Castle. Then the London police used her as a patrol horse from time to time. The mounted patrols in which she was used resulted in more than 250 arrests.

In 1987, when Burmese was twenty-five years old, Queen Elizabeth had ridden her in eighteen consecutive Birthday Parades. That year the queen retired the black mare.

Sergeant Robin Porter, who had looked after Burmese for the past six years, later wrote a letter about her. It was a tribute to the intelligent, good-natured black mare.

"I have been most fortunate having been asked to look after Burmese some six years ago," Sergeant Porter wrote. "A superb mare. I only wish she were ten years younger. She has never given me a moment's problem, and I do not suppose I shall ever have such a well-mannered, well-schooled, honest mount again. I have been associated with the preparation of royal horses for most of my service, and Burmese has certainly made my job easier."

After Queen Elizabeth retired Burmese, instead of using Centenial or any other horse, she no longer rode a horse in her Birthday Parades. She rode in a carriage, as she has done ever since.

In 1987, when the queen's open-top carriage arrived at the parade grounds, Burmese, ridden by Sergeant Porter, was already there. That year Queen Elizabeth wore summer clothing instead of the uniform of the regiment that was honouring her. She turned and looked from under her wide-brimmed summer hat at the black mare who had served her so well. Burmese stood quite still while the sergeant saluted the queen. As the royal carriage moved slowly past Burmese and her rider, the queen nodded toward them.

As soon as Burmese was retired, the queen gave orders that in future no-one was to ride her. The mare spent the rest of her life in a pasture at Windsor Castle. The queen choose that pasture so that when she spent time at the castle, she could look out of her window and see her long-time favourite mount.

In the early summer of 1990, Burmese died in the royal stables at Windsor Castle. Newspapers in Britain, in Canada, and elsewhere published news of the mare's death. One news item carried a photograph of Queen Elizabeth riding Burmese side-saddle in a Birthday Parade. The item noted that Burmese had been made famous through millions of such postcards showing her in royal ceremonies. Those who knew the mare could have added that she deserved all her fame.

Later Queen Elizabeth ordered a bronze statue of Burmese to be placed in the museum at Windsor Castle.

Author's Note

The Burmese story has been written as historical fiction. That is, most of it is true, but some people and minor events have been added.

The basic story of Burmese's rise, from an under-sized foal to leading file of the Musical Ride to Queen Elizabeth's favourite mount, is true.

Details of the RCMP ranch at Fort Walsh, of the riding school at Regina, and of the Musical Ride are also true. So are the long-time rumours that the RCMP would have to give up their horses. Burmese's experiences in England are also true.

Members of the RCMP are real, but some names have been changed. Real names have been used for ex-Commissioner S.T. Wood, Commissioner M.F.A. Lindsay, Inspector P.J.C. Morin, Staff Sergeant Ralph Cave, and Corporal Frede Rasmussen.

The Canadian Broadcasting Corporation broadcast only news-clips of the 1969 Birthday Parade.

Nora Hickson Kelly